THE CALL FOR THE MASTER

The late Karlfried Graf Dürckheim was acclaimed throughout Europe as the leading reconciler of Oriental and Western thought, as reflected in his numerous books. His best-known works are *The Way of Transformation: Daily Life as Spiritual Exercise, Zen and Us, The Japanese Cult of Tranquility, Hara: The Vital Centre of Man, The Grace of Zen,* and his most recently translated work, *Absolute Living* (also available in Arkana).

Born into the Bavarian nobility, he survived four years at the front in World War I and was saved at the last minute from a Spartacist firing squad during the abortive Bavarian Revolution of 1919. He later gave up his inheritance to undergo spiritual training as a psychologist and philosopher. Influenced by his association with Klee, Kandinsky, and Mies van der Rohe, his initiation into an esoteric group in Munich, and his studies with Heidegger, D. T. Suzuki, and others, he spent the Nazi years in Japan and went on to found the world-famous Center for Initiatory Psychotherapy in the Black Forest after World War II.

KARLFRIED GRAF DÜRCKHEIM

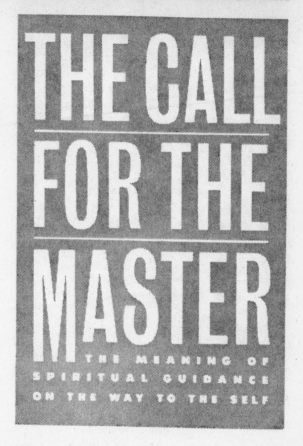

THE CALL FOR THE MASTER

THE MEANING OF SPIRITUAL GUIDANCE ON THE WAY TO THE SELF

Translated by Vincent Nash

PENGUIN

ARKANA

ARKANA
Published by the Penguin Group
Penguin Books USA Inc., 375 Hudson Street,
New York, New York 10014, U.S.A.
Penguin Books Ltd, 27 Wrights Lane, London W8 5TZ, England
Penguin Books Australia Ltd, Ringwood, Victoria, Australia
Penguin Books Canada Ltd, 10 Alcorn Avenue, Toronto, Ontario, Canada M4V 3B2
Penguin Books (N.Z.) Ltd, 182–190 Wairau Road, Auckland 10, New Zealand

Penguin Books Ltd, Registered Offices:
Harmondsworth, Middlesex, England

First published in the United States of America by E.P. Dutton, 1989
Published in Arkana Books 1993

1 3 5 7 9 10 8 6 4 2

Copyright © Scherz Verlag, Bern Munich, Vienna,
for Otto Wilhelm Barth-Verlag, 1975, 1986
Translation copyright © E. P. Dutton, 1989
All rights reserved

Originally published in West Germany under
the title *Der Ruf nach dem Meister.*

LIBRARY OF CONGRESS CATALOGING IN PUBLICATION DATA
Dürckheim, Karlfried Graf, 1896–
[Ruf nach dem Meister. English]
The call for the master: the meaning of spiritual guidance
on the way to the self/Karlfried Graf Dürckheim;
translated by Vincent Nash.
p. cm.
Translation of: Der Ruf nach dem Meister.
Bibliography: pp. 165–166.
ISBN 0 14 019.345 6
1. New Age movement. 2. Spiritual life. 3. Spiritual directors.
4. Self-realization. I. Title.
BP605.N48D8713 1989
291.6′1–dc19 88–23343

Printed in the United States of America
Set in REM Studio

Contents

MASTERS—STUDENTS—THE WAY

THE VOICE OF THE MASTER IN EVERYDAY LIFE

Preface

More and more often today, particularly among the young, the call is ringing out—the call for the master. This call is opening a new era in the history of the Western spirit.

In this call we hear the voice of a genuinely new era, superseding the earlier "modern age" that has long since ceased to be new. The call for the master is a sign that intellectual enlightenment is at last giving way to enlightenment of another sort—an enlightenment that helps Westerners see that intellectuality, so far their sole reference, actually seals them off from reality. A new door is opening.

The call for the master implies a farewell to old-style teachers and educators insofar as they claimed not merely to transmit knowledge and skills, but to turn out "right" people, leading "right" lives; for their notion of "rightness" lacked the one vital element: a commanding link with the *Absolute*, and the possibility the Absolute gives us of attaining the *maturity* that fulfills us as human beings. As long as we remain focused on success, achievement, and social conformity, our true humanity remains overshadowed and frustrated.

The old concept of human "rightness" is proving untenable, and so, for the same reason, is the ordinary notion of "reality," which has narrowed down to what we can perceive with our senses, know with our reason, order conceptually, and master technically. What this actually means is that only the rationally knowable is real! Everything else is fantasy, wishful thinking, emotion or belief—is, in other words, private, personal, and "merely subjective." This view of things leaves no room for the Absolute as the supra-worldly, transcendent reality of *Being,* infusing and molding our own lives.

One reason for the steady growth of the secular outlook is the mistaken belief that the Absolute no longer has anything to do with verifiable experience—a belief that the "champions of faith" and would-be empiricists of science have traditionally shared. In fact, the more "believers" look to revelation and deny that the Absolute can be experienced, the more they strengthen the position of the nonbelieving and supposedly empirical rationalists. Today, however, things are changing. Genuinely empirical scientists are increasingly having to admit not merely that there is a dimension in life that cannot be rationally grasped or causally explained but also that this dimension is an active, shaping presence. In the Christian camp, laymen and priests are both trying to find their way back to primal religious experiences, neglect of which is one of the reasons—as they themselves admit—for the decline of belief in our own day. But neither old-style psychologists and psychotherapists nor tradition-rooted priests and ministers can satisfy the turbulent and anguished longings of the young who, though alienated from "belief," nonetheless thirst for the Absolute and are bound by the shibboleths of neither science nor religion.

Today, supra-worldly reality is forcing its way irresistibly into human consciousness, demanding to be perceived in vital experience and expressed in responsible action. As incomprehensible energy and absolute conscience, "experience of the Absolute" has always been an unconscious element in living belief, but it has been concealed from rational consciousness. Today, the doors are beginning to open, and anyone who ventures through them enters a wholly new world—a world that the young are clamoring to reach. They know perfectly well that drugs are not the right way in. Who can show them what is? Who can show them the way?

The young are not alone in feeling the anguish of alienation from supra-worldly Being, and overcoming it depends, for both young and old, on specialized help, of which experience, vocation, knowledge, and maturity are the keynotes. They need a *master*—whether or not he already serves others in another capacity: as educator, psychologist, therapist, priest, or whatever.

To be a master—to live and work as a master in the world—is to bear effective witness to the Absolute that determines our lives. When we speak in this book of the Absolute, we mean the *true nature* of everything that is, which cannot be grasped and yet pervades our lives; divine *Being,* which transcends antitheses and space-time contingency; and *Life,* which lies beyond life and death. We mean universal true nature, in which we share individually in our own true nature, and we mean Life, from which and in which we live, Life that is constantly gathering us home to itself and releasing us back into the world, and that seeks to manifest itself in and through us in the world. When we speak of the Absolute, we are not basing ourselves on inherited belief, but on special experiences in which Being touches us in its supra-worldly fullness, order, and unity; in which it summons us, frees us—and imposes new obligations on us. In these experiences we encounter it in a direct, personal sense as a "you." Why do we not simply call it God? Because for people today who genuinely care and are genuinely searching, the renewal of religious life is rendered harder—even threatened—if the primal experience of the divine that they are looking for is confined within some concept of God or in those traditional theological formulas whose loss of substance has done so much to provoke the present crisis of belief. When we speak of the other dimension, of supra-worldly Life, divine Being, transcendent reality, or Life with a capital *L,* we are speaking all the time of an infinite *mystery.* Serving and bearing witness to that mystery is our purpose and destiny as human beings. This is why the master's true nature as witness and servant of Life can never be pinned down in concepts. We can only hint at what the term *master* implies. There is no linear, conceptual way of describing what he is and what he does. What he is, what emanates from him, what passes through him, what is sought in him—these are all questions that can at best be circled like some hidden, enigmatic center. From whatever angle the master is viewed and illuminated, his features and face are constantly changing. The same thing, however, is expressed in all of his forms. Obviously, this cyclical view—in which the one center is reflected from many different angles—involves saying the same thing more than once. These repetitions are basic formulas for the central element that shows through in every reflected image.

This book is not intended as a contribution to "human science," psychotherapy, or pedagogics, and it is not meant as an attack on theology or conventional pastoral care. It may, however, help those who have others in their charge to open up, in both themselves and those entrusted to their care, the true wellspring of Life, which threatens to run dry in our civilization and particularly in our schools and universities.

Our interest here is in rediscovering supra-worldly Life and in finding the way in which we can witness to it in the world. Both depend on the master.

Editorial Note: In this translation we have retained the pronoun *he* when referring to the master and the student, and in certain other cases to stress the singularity of individual experience. This reflects the author's original usage and is not meant as sex-specific.

The Call
for the Master

From Age to Age

The Archetypal Master

To be properly understood, human archetypes must always be related to their settings. They have specific meaning and value in a specific time and place. This is also true of masters.

The master's meaning differs from East to West—and the master has meant different things at different times in both East and West. Invariably associated with a religious tradition, he stands for something different in Buddhism, in Hinduism, and in Christianity. But just as the remoter religions would mean nothing to us unless every one expressed, in its own way, something intended for the whole of mankind, so we can speak of the master in general terms only because he has certain features whenever and wherever he appears.

Every human being is an individual manifestation of Life, which animates us all. In his own time, in his own place, in what he really is and in the stage he has reached, every human being is a specific element within the whole of divine Being, which is manifesting itself. In every one of us, Life appears in a unique form and a specific consciousness. In all its variations, however, whether revealing Being to a greater or lesser extent, the human condition expresses one idea: *humanity.* In the same way, the "idea of the master" runs through all historical manifestations as one of the ultimate ways in which humans can manifest divine Being in human form. "The master" means the expression in human form of "the Great Life"—Life that has made its way through all the barriers that in man's little life normally obscure and conceal it, Life come to fruition in a human; creative, redeeming. In the master, supra-worldly Life acquires for the human world a special self-manifesting and self-generating form.

The master is one of the archetypes of human Being. What does this mean?

There are certain root phenomena and sources, primal forms and basic figures of human life that are found wherever it appears. Human life is permanently tensioned between life and death, sense and absurdity, solitude and security, infancy and adulthood, the individual and the community. It oscillates all the time between departure and return, Yang and Yin, male and female, day and night, heaven and earth, conscious and unconscious.

Wherever there is human life there is generation and conception, promise and anguish, joy and sorrow, security and apprehension, protection and peril, satiety and hunger, waking and sleeping, sickness and healing. In all of these antitheses Life reveals itself.

Life in this sense is not an either/or, but something that transcends all antitheses and lives itself out in them. It is the whole that contains and surpasses them. It is the transcendent principle that manifests itself in the conflict and interplay of opposites, moving on from one form to the next in an everlasting pattern of change. But there is a secret order, a law, at the heart of life's fullness and unity. And so the same basic situations recur unceasingly—the same blind alleys, the same barriers, the same failures, and the same fresh beginnings and breakthroughs to further progress.

The range of human forms, of human energies and counterenergies, seems infinite, but human beings repeatedly appear in the same archetypal roles: as fathers, mothers, children, boys, girls, and also as farmers, craftsmen, soldiers, doctors, priests—the recurring components of human community.

Whenever human beings find themselves alone, they start looking for company. Whenever they are in trouble, they start looking for someone to help. Whenever they reach an impasse, they look for someone to show them the way out. Each of life's primal dilemmas is matched by its own saving power. Every recurrent anguish, longing, and hope finds its own special helper. The master is one of these helpers.

The archetypal master is the primal answer to a primal anguish that people encounter at a certain stage in their development. The master removes it by pointing the way to fulfillment of a promise felt within. In our day and age, more and more people are facing this anguish and are starting to sense this promise.

What anguish, what promise is at work here? What conflicts are resolved through the master's efforts, what destructive tests survived, what new life unleashed, what new way shown?

Linking Heaven and Earth

Our fundamental anguish is rooted in our twofold nature, the conflict between our earthly and heavenly origins, the pain of our exile in the world. The master embodies the promise of renewed union with otherworldly Being, and not simply in hope and in belief, but in real experience and on the path of transforming practice. Prehumans, like children today, were unaware of their twofold origin. Their divided nature was still contained within the primal One—and heaven and earth, the beyond and the here-and-now, were still conjoined in the harmony of Life. But sooner or later this harmony was inevitably shattered.

As far as we can tell, humans everywhere have always experienced their own existence in the tension between two realities: the reality that their own experience and the experiences and traditions of others have made more or less familiar, and with which they feel more or less at home; and something mysteriously present within this familiar, everyday reality, something that cannot be grasped and controlled in the same way—that cannot be touched and yet touches their own life profoundly. All the time there is another reality beyond their reach—unpredictable, benevolent, and menacing by turns— on which natural powers have no hold.

Certain human beings have always been accounted superior because they have clearly had privileged links with this other dimension and have seemingly been able to contact higher forces—knowing perhaps how to dispose them in humanity's favor or win their goodwill with special practices and sacrifices. For whether it threatens or assists, this second reality has always been recognized as the more powerful of the two. It was and has remained the transcendent and ultimate reference, both as basic threat to existence and as hope and guiding promise of a better life, a life without suffering. But the behavior of these "powers" has always seemed to relate in some way to human behavior. And so the problem has always been how to make the right kind of contact with them, how to share in their power, how to accede to the happiness they can give. What is the way that leads to contact, and perhaps even union, with the second, supra-worldly reality? On countless levels and in countless ways, depending on spiritual maturity and individual tradition, human beings have always attempted to understand the supernatural, win its favor, and reach it themselves. The vast variety of their religions is itself one proof of this.

Whatever specific religions may have taught and whatever the part played in them by faith, live religious feeling in the long term has always depended on one thing only—the believer's personal experience of the divine and his or her ability to achieve union with it. The same three questions have always been asked: What way? What price? What "practice"? They are aimed at someone who knows the way and can lead others on it. They reflect the age-old longing for someone to bridge the gap between earth and heaven. The eternal longing for an end to the primal tension between here-and-now, contingent life and otherworldly Life, divine Being, is still with us—expressed in the call for the master.

From Primal Fear to Inside Knowledge

There is a vast difference between the life instinct of people who feel themselves the helpless playthings of demonic forces and try to propitiate them with prayers and offerings, either personally or through a go-between, and belief in a personal God whose love frees the world from the power of evil.

Similarly, the development from forms of life and consciousness that are rooted in magic and myth through mental consciousness to integrated consciousness, in which all the previous stages are present and compounded, is a tremendous one.* And there is a massive difference between the human being seen as a dust speck in the cosmos and the human being seen as the microcosm of the universe, sensing in himself the promise of being able consciously to express, in himself and

*Cf. Jean Gebser, *The Ever-Present Origin* (Athens: Ohio University Press, 1985).

through himself, the fullness of the whole in a way that is human and superhuman at once.

What a difference there is between a fear-ridden vision of destiny, in which outside forces are seen as the only enemy, and the vision that teaches us to seek the enemy of fulfillment in ourselves. It is the difference between the medicine man, who placates far-off gods with gory offerings, and the person who bridges the gap between this world and the next within himself; the difference between seeing suffering and sorrow only as the enemies of life, and seeing them as helping us move toward union with something above us and "beyond"—not only this life, but life and death as well.

Different ways of seeing the relationship between this world and the next reflect different levels and degrees of human consciousness of *Life*. So, nowadays, does the difference between people who are prisoners of tangibles, facts and objective experience, and people who can recognize and attend to what only the inner eye can see; between people for whom nothing is real unless objective consciousness can grasp it and technique control it, and people who experience transcendence as the only true reality. This latter view pertains to subjective consciousness only. It cannot be understood and it cannot be mastered, but knowledge of it is the essential precondition of everything a master does. In tangible reality, it is more concealed than manifest. It reveals itself only to the inner eye.

Today there are clearly two distinct groups: one is content to progress by acquiring worldly knowledge, skills, and savoir faire; the other looks beyond this to an inner maturing toward the true self, a process that neither depends on nor provides an increase in worldly knowledge, skill, and possessions, but aims at closer contact with supra-worldly Being. This requires a different kind of knowledge, a knowledge that is based on a special kind of experience, penetrates the mystery of Being, and bears within itself the way that leads to Being. It is "initiatory" knowledge. To "initiate" means to open the way to the mystery.* This knowledge is possessed, transmitted, and made effective by masters.

Timeless Knowledge—The Great Tradition

There is here-and-now knowledge and there is timeless knowledge. The knowledge that helps us to master the world is increasing all the time. Each new discovery treads hard on its predecessor's heels, and yesterday's is no longer good enough today. In the knowledge of a Lao-tse, however, there is a wisdom that is as valid today as it was in his own lifetime.

There is, in humanity's body of wisdom about our inner development and relationship with the otherworldly, a vital element that has nothing to do with space and time, something that is both revealed and concealed in worldly phenomena and contradictions—although transcendent Life shines through every outer shell. This otherworldly element constitutes the true nature of everything that is; it is eternally valid, hidden, and yet omnipresent for those with eyes to see it; it is contained in an innate primal knowledge and conscience that human beings can bring to consciousness. The truth embodied in it lives in the Great Tradition, itself timeless, running through all places and all times.

The concern of the Great Tradition is with primal knowledge, repeatedly renewing itself in experience, of the conditions under which Being has been concealed in humanity, and the conditions under which it can again take form in the world, in and through human beings. We meet it in the enlightened knowledge of great sages and masters, and as the kernel of the creation myths and salvific longings of all the great religions.

*Cf. J. Evola, "Über das Initiatische," *Antaios,* vol. VI/2 (1964).

The Great Tradition expresses the truth of other-worldly Life as it repeatedly comes to the light of consciousness, forcing its way through multiple distortions toward worldly fulfillment in humanity. The Great Tradition is the story of divine Being, lost to and seeking itself, obscured in the contingent, in rebellious matter, in the contradictions of mortal creation, and above all, in human consciousness, but able, because its spark is inextinguishably preserved in humanity's true nature, to wake and find itself again in human beings—irradiated now by a new consciousness. Initiatory knowledge and the actions of the masters inspired by it are rooted in the truth of this past and future story. In it are resolved all the antitheses that divide human beings, in here-and-now contingency, into areas, races, characters, and stages of development and consciousness. Also resolved is the difference between East and West.

There seems at first to be an unbridgeable gap between the Western affirmation of form, personality, and the historicity of our existence, and the Eastern view of life, which more or less rejects all of this and ultimately seeks the truth in the formless, impersonal, and ahistorical *All-One*. But there is a higher truth in which the East/West antithesis appears as a tension in ourselves (that is, as a natural part of being human), and the contradictions are seen as the polar sources of a dialectical tension that sustains the living whole in different ways, depending on which of the two extremes is dominant. In this way, differences in temperament and outlook can be seen as shifts in polar emphasis. It is only at this point that a genuine encounter between East and West, and also between Christianity and Buddhism, becomes really meaningful; for this view helps each side to improve its understanding of the other and to emphasize its own special features in a better-informed and more fruitful manner. The forms in which Life's primal truth reveals itself are always contingent and thus different, but its inner nature is above all antitheses—and this truth is alive in every master. This is also why the real masters of all spiritual traditions transmit something of universal validity.

Sages and Masters

The primal truth of Life can take human form in two figures: the sage and the master. They are genuine historical figures only when the depths of otherworldly Being have utterly *made them over.* At that point they both know that, although surrounded by the world's limitations, they are basically subject to none of them. They have overcome the ground notes of human existence: fear, despair, and desolation.

The master is the sage in whom Life is active not only as a power that transforms and raises him personally to a higher stage of human development but also as a power that enables him to effect this transformation in others. The master does not simply know—he acts as well. In both master and sage, absolute Life is not simply a matter of inner knowledge or living belief—it is present as an ongoing process of realization and change. In the master, the otherworldly is present as experience, illuminated by knowledge, and active as a transforming force.

In addition to sages and masters, there is always a third category—people in whom Life comes to consciousness chiefly in the form of *knowledge.* They are "great knowers," men and women of learning (corresponding to the Indian *Pandits*), but not conventional scholars, because their interest is in things that can be known but not understood. Without being totally transformed themselves, they can communicate "esoteric knowledge" to others. This means that they must have something of both the sage and master, but they live as seekers and researchers, buried in secret things, in hidden laws, in the primal meaning of images. Perhaps Carl Jung was one of these.

Both sages and masters exist on a higher plane than ordinary mortals. Although human, they live on a superhuman level. If we can nonetheless sense something of their true nature and significance, this is because there is something in every one of us that, as promise, primal knowledge, and responsibility, also transcends the normally human: the inner master! Deep inside each of us is also potentially the great knower, sage, and master. An awareness of this potential is spreading today. It is the radiant and positive force behind the process of inner change that the Western spirit is now undergoing; the checking of this potential is the dark and negative counterforce.

Today, traditional standards are being rejected more radically than ever before, and in a different sense. The confrontation today is not simply between those who focus solely on the world and try to master reality rationally and technically, and those who seek religious fulfillment in the inwardness of a world-rejecting belief. The real conflict is now between both of these groups and those who are trying to experience, anchor, and give form to the reality of the divine in the world and the truth of the worldly in God. The traditional conflict between faith and knowledge is a thing of the past. It belongs to a stage of human consciousness that the advanced spirits of our age are already overcoming. Indeed, all the great masters of the past, including the great Christian masters, had already moved beyond it. The longing to experience the Absolute within and, changing, to become what true nature wants us to be, is something that unites all serious seekers. To satisfy this longing has always been the master's task. For people in the West, however, there is only one possible master: not a master who decides the conflict of inwardness and world in favor of an inwardness that entirely neutralizes the worldly, but a master who resolves it in a way that allows "spirit to become flesh," allows the world's true nature to fulfill itself from the supra-worldly in all its multiform, here-and-now complexity.

In Our Own Day

The Question

What can I do to bring back the thing I have experienced—no, what can I do to stay in touch with it?

What was this experience?

I don't know—I only know that it knocked me sideways—everything in me is still trembling.

Was it beautiful? Was it good?

It was much more than beautiful or good. It was simply IT!

What do you mean, "IT"?

The only thing that matters. It was overpowering, massive—I can't tell you—fullness, light, love—all together.

Quite an experience!

Much more than that—"experience" sounds so subjective. It was much more. There was something there—I don't know who or what—I felt a presence—

And you—?

I was suddenly a new person, totally free, entirely myself and in myself and yet connected with everything. I had forgotten everything and yet I knew everything. I felt so strong—and inconceivably happy. For a moment, I was totally myself—no, not "myself" at all, and yet more myself than I had ever been, and much, much more.

What were you doing when it happened?

Nothing. It came out of nowhere, grabbed me, knocked me over, drained me, filled me, drove me into myself, pulverized me, brought me back to myself, and carried me beyond myself—I can't tell you what it was like.

Were you confused? Did things look different?

Confused? Not for a second! Clearer than I'd ever been before. And more than clear—I saw things I'd never seen before.

What?

I could look into things and through them—see what they "really" were. I can't describe it. Everything suddenly meant some-

thing completely different. Everything was totally itself and much more—completely different and completely itself because of the difference.

And you?

Just the same! Completely different, a whole new person, and totally myself because of the difference. I no longer belonged to myself.

And now?

Yes, and now! Now I want someone to explain it all to me. No—what's the point of explaining!—to tell me I'm right, to take the whole thing on and, even more, tell me what to do. I know that's the way to it!

To what?

The meaning. The purpose. The reason why we're here at all. I need someone who's been through it, who "knows" and . . .

Who Is Looking for Masters?

Thousands of people are talking like this today. But who are they? Most of them are people who have felt something new break in, something that touches them on the deepest level—something mysterious and incomprehensible that fills them with joy but imposes obligations on them, that is charged with promise and will not let them go. And now they need someone who knows what they are talking about and can help them to change and live in the way their experience demands! They are looking for masters.

The master is the answer to a question that we ask in a specific inner situation, but ask only when we have reached a particular stage in our development. We often ask it because we have come to a dead end, have reached some extreme of inner anguish where our own wisdom and strength are no longer enough and where even our religious beliefs can do nothing more to help us. Often we sense and are looking for something that is meant for and entrusted to us on the deepest level—something that could finally bring us fulfillment. We sense it because we have had a very special kind of experience.

Somehow we have made contact with the otherworldly, with the divine, in a way that forces us to look into ourselves and direct our future steps on a new path. We do not ourselves know what has really happened—we only know that it is vital to make lasting contact with whatever has touched us. And so we start looking for someone who can show us how to do this. We know that neither father, mother, doctor, teacher, psychotherapist, nor even priest can help. Who can? This question points straight to the master.

Who Asks the Question?

The question is often asked by young people who have never had any beliefs and who suddenly experience something that knocks the ground from under them—and opens up entirely new horizons. Many of them have "thought"—also lived and acted, destroyed, and even killed—as militant atheists, materialists, Communists, Maoists, and now suddenly experience something that hits them like a thunderbolt, smashing their worldview to atoms in an instant. Suddenly it all falls apart, and they start asking new questions and searching in a wholly new direction.

It is often asked by people—in all walks of life and of all levels of education—who have given up their beliefs but increasingly have the uneasy feeling that "something is missing." Not content with turning their backs on their churches, they repress every trace and reminder of their childhood beliefs—for fear of falling back into them. This also means, however, that they are stifling everything that still gets through and touches them in a direct and numinous sense. In the long run, this can only lead to trouble. The strain increases and, when they can finally bear it no longer, they start looking for someone to, as they say, "put them back in touch"—but not in the old way!

It is often asked, too, by those unfortunates whom radical psychoanalysis has not simply freed from a pseudo-God but actually rendered incapable of hearing Being's call. Many of them, including numerous Freudians, are themselves former analysts whom analysis has robbed of more than belief. For years they have held religion at arm's length in their work—only to sense increasingly that, deep down, something is wrong. Their training has taught them to be honest with themselves, and this honesty now forces them to admit that what they are feeling is guilt. Eventually, the pressure can build to an intensity that sends them looking for someone who can secretly open a new door and lead them into the buried depths.

It is often asked by old people, who are at last beginning to loosen the chains with which they hold (and are held by) the thousands of things that have made up their world. One day grace suddenly touches them and they start to think: "If only I could let everything go, everything could still be different." This mood can be the product of solitude and calm, but it can also come after a blazing family quarrel, when people cemented in the ego use age itself as a weapon against their intimates, become furious, rage against them—and collapse. Suddenly, they feel admitted to a great freedom, a freedom that comes from a new and unknown source. What has happened? Who can explain it? Who can make this new happiness secure?

It is sometimes asked by people who have tried to take their own lives. At the very moment of death, when the poison was starting to work, or just after they surfaced, when the ego was still not fully present, they found themselves in another world. Liberated from their worldly egos, they experienced their own true natures and a mighty freedom. This unparalleled experience still works and vibrates in them now. They sense that the jewel and secret of life has been offered them, but have no idea what to do with it or how to hang on to it. And so they start looking for someone to tell them what this tremendous experience means and how to preserve it, deepen it, and make it fruitful.

Today, it is being asked by many young people who have experienced ecstatic states with the help of drugs—blissful moments of immensity and total release. Somewhere beyond the world's conceptual limitations and taboos, they have been in touch with something that lives on in them afterward as "real." They are left with the unshakable conviction that they have actually experienced something that lies outside the banalities of everyday experience and is more "rewarding" than any experience that everyday consciousness can offer them. But then the problems start. They lose confidence in the means, the drug that gave them this experience. Was it the wrong way in? Are there others? Who can open up the right one?

There are also tough executives, industrialists, and politicians who have been brought by failure, actual or imminent, into contact with something new and "strange." At the very moment when their power and status were crumbling, something new surfaced within them—something wonderful and overwhelmingly good from deep inside themselves. What was it? They are embarrassed to speak of it to others and remain secretly ashamed long afterward that "that kind of thing" could have "got to" them. They cannot really bring themselves to trust the inner voice that is telling them: "That's it—that's what it's really about." But the voice persists, and they eventually start looking for someone who knows what it means and can help them to take the next step.

The question is also asked today by many priests and ministers. They are true to their beliefs, are tireless pastors in caring for others, lead holy lives of work and prayer in their communities, say Mass or conduct worship regularly—and yet their real contact with the divine has been lost; sometimes they have even lost the ability to pray. It is as if they are dried out. They sense that they are living a lie—and suffer from this feeling. They are ashamed of seeming something that they are not, and are racked by inner torment and anguish. And then, one day, the "other dimension" bursts in on them—perhaps as they peel an apple or when a stone in the garden makes them stumble—and they momentarily experience themselves in the fullness of Being! They are left confronting a riddle and often, too, a frightening question: How can this experience be made to square with their religious system? For the first time they feel the difference between belief and experience, and are left wondering how they themselves can reconcile the two. Why have their beliefs, the beliefs they have lived by, not given them long ago the indescribable sense of liberation and joy they have just experienced? Perhaps they have sought the spring of salvation too far "outside" themselves? And then they start looking for someone to help them forward, for instinct tells them that some inner process of development, maturity, and change still awaits them, and that this depends on something other than pious contemplation, fidelity to their beliefs, and "steadfastness in faith."

Anyone who has had an experience like this and been given the grace not to betray and shrug it off as mere emotion, who has avoided slotting it into a ready-made "system" and has taken it seriously just as it is, is on the threshold of something that offers him or her a fundamentally and genuinely new possibility of living meaningfully. Far more people than we imagine have come to this threshold today. Many of them become physically sick when they fail to cross it. Life is bottled up in them and struggling to get out, choked aggression fills them, they fall into depression and no longer know which way to turn—although the light of the original experience still flickers dimly deep inside. The next step comes when they start looking for someone who knows the way out of the impasse and into a new life. Who can they turn to? Not a doctor, who has no professional knowledge in this field, probably admits as much—and only prescribes tranquilizers or recommends a psychiatrist. Psychologists and psychotherapists, on the other hand, may trace the most precious experience they have ever had "back" to something else or write it off as illusion, fantasy, or wish fulfillment. The most painful and damaging thing that can happen in this situation is to fall into the hands of someone who has never had an experience like this and so misinterprets it—declaring, for example, that an experience of God, which can indeed make a person behave "abnormally" for a short time, is an instance of "mania." With priests and pastors, there is always the risk that theological orthodoxy will make them cast doubt on the experience, dismiss it as merely "natural" and "subjective," and even try to lead someone who has turned to them for help and advice back into the arms of Mother Church (back, in other words, to the very stage that had just seemed outgrown). What is really needed is an entirely different kind of helper—the master.

The Experience That Triggers the Call for the Master

There are many different types and levels of experience and situation that trigger the call for the master. Sometimes, when we are ready, the gentlest of contacts with Being is enough to wake a sudden and powerful longing for union with the Great Unknown. Sometimes it takes a "mighty experience," an experience of shattering power, that brings the other dimension personally home beyond all doubt as liberation, promise, and obligation. Sometimes it is an ultimate crisis, in which we have totally exhausted our resources of wisdom and strength, have really come to the end—particularly when we have also lost all religious belief.

The first contact with Being can come from an encounter with another person; from a word, a question, a gesture, a look that pierces through and through—and suddenly it happens. Without the slightest warning, something new breaks into our life and a secret decision is taken, a decision that may be completely unconscious to start with.

The trigger can be a sentence in a book, a new idea, or even some phrase repeatedly heard or read. Suddenly a mighty bell booms out and, in the listener, a commanding note rings out in powerful, unmistakable reply.

It can also be something completely trivial, a minor mishap, a twisted ankle, a fever fantasy, the sight of children playing. It may be a dream, a sexual experience, a scene in a film, or, nowadays, a drug high—in all these cases a different reality is glimpsed and we suddenly feel that another world is calling. These experiences, if they remain fruitfully operative afterward, all share certain features: a numinous quality and the sense of otherworldly power, obligation and promise in the experience of immanent transcendence. Of course, we are not necessarily conscious of these features as such, but they are all part of the experience that turns life around and gives it new direction. To have it we must have matured, without knowing it, into readiness for a process that cannot be "induced" or made to happen from our normal ego. What this process involves is opening ourselves to the Absolute; it depends on tearing down the wall that cuts us off from the divine. This wall is our whole accustomed context, is our old ego with its unshakable habits of thought and its hardened demand for a quiet life, obvious meanings, and personal security—all of it wrapped up in the firm framework of the familiar. This wall, which cuts us off from genuine maturity and change, can be broken through, and we can allow this to happen, but we cannot take credit for doing it, for this is not something that we "do" ourselves. An outside force breaks in and comes to meet us. This outside force is grace, and it comes from another dimension so totally different from anything we experience in the world that we can only call it otherworldly. What we experience here goes beyond our world-centered, self-centered ego, and yet comes from a reality that is plainly within us—the reality of our *true nature*. This true nature is nothing less than the mode in which supra-worldly Being is permanently present within us and seeking to manifest itself, in and through us, in the here-and-now. Its irruption into the everyday world is grace, but we must be capable of allowing it to act and we can prepare for it! This is where spiritual exercise comes in.

The experience that triggers the call for the master is always an encounter with our true nature, in which the Absolute breaks into consciousness. It comes without warning and defies comprehension, but its impact and the joy it brings are sufficient to make us start looking for someone who can link us to it permanently in a manner that both matches the truth of what we are and allows us to meet the world on its own terms.

In most cases, the freedom and joy that a person's first contact with supra-worldly Being brings are also a saving answer to the three fundamental problems that darken human life and that the natural ego can neither endure nor accept: *annihilation, meaninglessness,* and *solitude.*

Annihilation, either physical or social, can "frighten us to death." Similarly, absurdity can be felt so utterly as disillusionment, disorder, and injustice that it destroys all the beliefs and obliterates all the meanings by which we live, driving us to the edge of insanity and toppling us into despair. And the death of a loved one, the treachery of friends, exclusion from the community—all of these can create a loneliness beyond our strength. But in extremities like these, where the unacceptable—imminent death, ultimate absurdity, or total isolation—can no longer be avoided, we may be given the strength to do something that the natural ego cannot do: accept the unacceptable. We may accept it only for a split second, but this is enough—enough for a crack to open briefly in the carapace of our limitations and to let the limitless stream in. And true nature, which embodies the supra-worldly, suddenly lifts us to a different level. We have experienced the miracle: by accepting annihilation we have found a *life* beyond life and death, a life that has left annihilation behind; by accepting meaninglessness we have found a *meaning* beyond meaning and unmeaning; and by humbly accepting isolation we have found a *security* beyond security and isolation as the world understands those terms. In other words, we have experienced ourselves in indwelling transcendence, in what we truly are: a person who shares in supra-personal, universal Life, and to whom Life has revealed itself—in its fullness as absolute strength, in its order as absolute meaning, and in its unity as absolute love.

These experiences are so powerful that it is hard to understand why "metanoia" (conversion) does not follow for everyone who has them. But is anyone really prepared and able to meet these experiences in the right way? Is anyone even prepared and able to take them seriously? Today, at last, people are. Nowadays people know the limitations of rational knowledge, are tired of superficial pleasures, are starting to reject the one-sided emphasis on performance and success and to long for something totally different—something they must find. At last, too, they are ready for the experience in which their true nature is freed and they meet the Absolute, not merely as a free-floating abstraction, but as a power that relieves worldly anguish and, lifting them onto a new level, both promises everything and imposes certain obligations.

When supra-worldly Being, divine Life—what Christian believers would call Christ or God—bursts into consciousness at moments like this, the whole experience is so incomprehensible, startling, and overpowering that "ordinary," unprepared men and women simply do not know what to make of it, even wondering whether they have lost their reason. In most cases, the mighty wave that has lifted them for an instant dies out on the sands of natural doubt. But not always—increasingly, there are people who are hit so hard that the experience marks them for good, people who then start calling for the master.

Nowadays, one has the impression that it is chiefly the young, and not older people, who are looking for and waking to their true selves. There seem to be more and more young people in whom the membrane separating them from their true nature is so thin, and the power with which their true nature is struggling to the surface so great, that the merest touch can provoke a breakthrough that is often dangerous.

Some minute change is enough to make the form forced on them by the world—a form at odds with their true nature—collapse. The result may *look* like schizophrenia. The young man or woman suddenly starts spouting nonsense, claims to be Jesus Christ, or turns violent and begins hitting out—and seems ripe for the psychiatric clinic. If he or she actually lands in such a clinic and is seen or treated as a lunatic, then one of life's decisive opportunities may well have been wasted; for these were the symptoms of true nature breaking through, true nature that should have been guided carefully into the right channels. The force that surges to the surface in these tragic cases is often hard to control, but it reflects a situation in which many people find themselves today. They are ready to cross into a new realm, and they need someone who knows enough to lead them bravely, carefully, and understandingly into the true life that is their destiny.

Where Do We Find Masters?

Where are the masters we are looking for today? Masters are at home in the Oriental tradition, but are not an automatic and central part of our social fabric in the West. Why not? Obviously because the existential question answered by masters has never arisen in the West with sufficient force to encourage or even compel them to appear. What are the reasons for this?

Generally speaking, people in the West are more involved with the world, and people in the East more concerned with inner growth. Westerners feel a stronger urge to tackle the world head-on and test their powers on it. They have faith in the reality of the here-and-now and believe that shaping the world is their appointed task. To assert themselves in the world, achieve something in it, and give it valid form in what they make—these are their natural instincts and the things they feel destined to do. To do them, knowledge, skills, self-discipline, and good behavior seem sufficient. And what of the anguish within? To a limited extent, this is acknowledged and subsumed in redemptive belief; but remaining true to one's beliefs is not necessarily a sign of maturity! It is true, of course, that inner anguish can dissolve in a sense of being shielded by a benevolent divinity, in peace of spirit, and in the promise of redemption into a higher life beyond this world. People in whom this belief is living, effective, and dominant have no interest in the inner way, the way of initiation, or in the master who shows them how to follow it.

In all but a few cases the two traditional pillars of existence in the West—exploring and shaping the world, and secure beliefs—have left two things undeveloped: responsible awareness of the fact that inner maturity is something that we can and should attain, and responsible awareness of the fact that there is an inner development process that we can and should undergo and that allows us to *experience,* in a broadened consciousness, something hitherto possessed only as a pious belief. This is why many leading public figures—business people, politicians, and even priests and ministers—are incredibly lacking in true maturity and wholly fail to see that something is missing. They are unfocused, ego-centered, authoritarian, unfree, wary of criticism, angst-ridden, emotional, and lonely. This shows that they lack sustaining contact and a permanent link with their own true nature. It is precisely in this contact, however, that the life-wisdom of the East (and not only of the East) is rooted. And the fact that the East sees its cultural triumphs not in objects and artifacts but in its sages clearly illustrates the difference between two views of life and their practical effects. One of the symptoms of the immaturity of even educated Westerners is their failure to throw off the universal shackles of objective consciousness. And one of the results of failing to develop their consciousness is being shut off from true nature and the transcendent *experience* that reveals it. This deficiency is itself a threat to belief. For, when belief is questioned by reason and touched by doubt, only the experience of true nature rooted in transcendence can renew it utterly.

The difference between East and West can be really and fruitfully grasped only if it is seen not as a matter of folk or national psychology but as a basic human problem. "Experience of the Absolute" and the way of initiation (of which that experience is starting point, focus, and destination) are both integral features of the Eastern tradition of masters—and they are as much of a potential in Westerners as Easterners. In the West they have simply been overshadowed by beliefs founded on revelation and by a sense of the need to shape and master the world, and so have not appeared forcefully. The time has now come for them to do so—and do so they will. To make this possible, we must stop relying solely on "objective values," stop dismissing human feelings and instinctive concerns as "merely subjective," and see every human as a "subject" whose maturity and fulfillment depend on something more than a talent for surviving and "doing a good job."

Just as one cannot mature to one's true self unless one is in touch with one's real center, one's true nature, which is not determined by the world, so the coming of this real center to inner consciousness, as we are experiencing it today, expresses itself in a longing for true selfhood and for guidance on the way to this goal. Once the anguish of failing to fulfill our true nature becomes conscious, neither worldly success nor a return to belief can remove it, because it actually springs from a situation in which ordinary achievement no longer provides fulfillment and beliefs no longer offer support. And so the longing for guidance on the inner way cannot be ignored.

But supposing no masters are available—what then? There are three answers.

First, anyone whom true anguish has driven to the edge always finds the master! It is a strange fact of human experience that great suffering generates its own remedy. Again and again, people driven by despair to seek the counsel and help demanded by their true nature themselves construct the helpers they need, simply because they are suffering and searching so intensely. They receive a master's answer or a master's guidance from others who are by no means masters themselves. Responding from the innermost depths of their humanity, these others speak, almost without thinking, to the questioner's own anguished inner depths—and give the right answer. In fact, it is not they who are giving the answer: it is revealed to them and they simply pass it on. The need of the one and the readiness of the other have stretched a mysterious string between them—and the bow is wielded and the saving note sounded by some third force. It is thus true to say that anyone can act as our master if we call him or her in the right way.

Second, there are far more people than we suppose whose own development and experience would fit them to act as masters if they only knew that they had those qualities and trusted them. Those with long experience in counseling and caring (psychotherapists, for example) always include some who could take others at least part of the way if they were only aware of the dimension that concerns us here and were willing to take on the possibilities and duties that go with it—had, in other words, the courage to take the step from therapist to guru. Of course, the qualifications required are not the ones conventionally involved in training for the counseling and caring professions. What teacher, doctor, or priest has ever been taught, for example, that there is an inner person, that this inner person has a duty to seek maturity and can achieve genuine selfhood through contact with his or her true nature and the Absolute within it? So far, modern therapy has concentrated solely on pragmatic healing and relieving worldly suffering; that is, the suffering we feel when we fail to meet the world's demands. But who can cure the other kind of suffering, the suffering we feel when we fail to meet the demands of true nature? Who knows about the suffering that comes from being separated from our true nature and the Absolute within it? This is the suffering that really typifies our age. Initiation is the keynote of the only healing that can cure it, and the purpose of initiation in this sense is learning how to be reunited with our true nature, to stay united with it, and to live from it.* To help us on this path, however, therapists must have the qualities of the guru and master! In this day and age, they have a positive duty to acquire those qualities!

And yet the most important answer to the question "Where do we find masters?" is "In ourselves"—for there is such a thing as the *inner* master.

*Cf. Maria Hippius, "Am Faden von Zeit und Ewigkeit," in *Transzendenz als Erfahrung,* ed. M. Hippius (Weilheim: O. W. Barth-Verlag, 1966).

Masters—Students—
the Way

The Master—Idea and Reality

The Eternal Master

The word *master* means three things: the eternal master, the here-and-now master, the inner master.

The eternal master is a principle perceived in a primal image, an idea, an archetype. The here-and-now master is the living embodiment of that principle in a given time and place. The inner master is the possibility—individually sensed as promise, potential, and obligation—of giving the eternal master physical form and reality in one's own life.

As idea, person, or inner obligation, *the master* always signifies Life become human—otherworldly Life manifesting itself in the world in human form.

The master exists only in relation to a person who is totally absorbed in the quest for Life's Way to this form—the student. And so there can be no master without the Way and without a student.

The idea behind the word *master* is that of the *homo maximus,* the universal man or woman, in whom Being—Life in its totality, as fullness, order, and unity—manifests itself in human form and, changing and creating, works itself out in the world in a way that both transcends the world and masters it. For students, the true master realizes the idea that has woken in them as the inner master (as potential and obligation), the idea that they hope and intend to realize themselves on the way shown them by the master.

Like the master, the student and the Way also exist in three senses: as idea, actuality, and inner truth.

It is in the threefold unity of master, student, and Way that absolute, otherworldly Being overcomes all resistance and limitations and takes on form in our here-and-now world. Our duty and destiny as human beings is to prepare ourselves increasingly to play a part in this process; that is, to obey Life's urge to manifest itself in the world and cooperate with it. It is only at a certain stage in our development that we can achieve awareness of Life and recognize it in this sense, consciously accepting that our central obligation is to help it manifest itself and advancing on the "way" this realization reveals to us.

In the past, peoples and individuals have realized the ideas of master, student, and Way in many different forms, depending on their character, maturity, and spiritual traditions. Every one of these forms has expressed an archetypal triunity imprinted in human nature—eternal master, eternal student, eternal way.

Our notion of Life is essentially conditioned by the way we experience and perceive the relationship between absolute and contingent reality. If we see Being as the one true reality and ourselves as the prisoners of the world, then the only way of fulfilling ourselves and getting back in touch with that ultimate reality is to leave the world utterly behind, die, and so finally enter the reality of All-One-Being. If, on the other hand, we see Life as transcending the antithesis of otherworldly Being and worldly reality, and manifestation of the

Absolute in the worldly as our real objective, then we fulfill ourselves by witnessing to it in our ways of living, learning, and acting in the world. And so there are two fundamentally different ways in which true Life manifests, fulfills, and consummates itself. The first step is common to both—death, dissolution of the world-hardened, world-centered, here-and-now ego in Being, beyond space and time. The thrust and purpose of the process differ, however, depending on whether the human condition is ultimately denied and left behind or is consciously accepted as the ultimate manifestation of divine Being. The law of the spirit made flesh applies in the Judeo-Christian West. And this is why the idea of masters ultimately means something different in East and West.

The eternal master is Life, Life lost to itself in objective consciousness, trying to find itself again and seeking to manifest itself in the world—as fullness that sustains and nurtures every living thing, as order that regulates the coming of everything to form, and as unity that allows every living thing to become one with itself and everything else and is constantly creating wholeness anew. Life can manifest itself only in a neverending process of dying and becoming. In the master, it appears in pure form as the principle of eternal change. The whole point of change is the person who successfully fulfills his or her destiny by witnessing to Life in his or her physical existence. The eternal master intervenes when our persistence in preventing Life, present in our true nature, from manifesting itself has gone beyond a certain point and created a situation we can no longer endure.

Our true nature is the mode in which otherworldly Life is individually present within us and seeking to manifest itself, in and through us, in the world. In this true nature, we always remain the children of Life—Life that reveals itself in everlasting change—and this is why the barriers raised against it, without our knowledge, by our defining consciousness, involve us in a typically human type of anguish. When it builds to a certain intensity, this anguish finally enables us to hear the voice of our disregarded true nature. We hear it in many different ways: in depression and sickness, unexpected turns in our own lives, windfalls and disasters, strange meetings and "coincidences" in which Life appears to be moving against the things that stop it from emerging. We also hear it, however, in a growing thirst for something new, in anxiety and optimism, in an unfocused longing for freedom, in a sense of the numinous, in fleeting contacts with Being, and at last, also in certain "mighty experiences" that shock us into consciousness and tell us that the time has come to change our lives completely. This is when we need the master.

Two things can take us over the threshold that leads to the master: suffering and promise. Suffering is always the result of standing still or going astray on the way we are meant to follow, of offending against the inner wholeness that seeks to realize its own totality and depends on constant change. The inner promise first comes home to us when the ultimate source of true selfhood, the life-stream from our true nature, swells until it threatens, in one liberating act, to sweep away the barriers of objective consciousness; suddenly we wake to the sense of a greater life within us that is merely waiting to be let in. It is at moments like this that the Absolute, present within us as a latent creative force, can defeat the contingent in an instant. When this happens, a new conscience is born— and the inner master, who embodies Life, awakes!

The Inner Master

There are always two levels on which master and student cooperate in bringing Being into existence in human shape: one is the external, contingent world, where master and student meet as real human beings—and the other is within the seeker himself. The master here is not an outside figure but an authority directing the student from within. Deep inside ourselves, we are all masters and students in this sense, and this is due to the anguish and strength of true nature, forcing its way within us toward self-realization in worldly form. But we

34

must bring this fact to consciousness. Seeking and finding the external master depend, like everything that master does, on the inner master.

People who have matured to the Way and are looking for a master to guide them, but who cannot find the master they need near at hand, should know that they carry a master—the inner master—in themselves. Otherwise they could never find an outer master—would not recognize him even if they met him. As Goethe put it in *Xenien:* "And were the eye not of the sun, it never could the sun descry." Nor, if they had no inner master, could an "outer" master do anything for them.

We can find and accept outside masters only if, deep down in our true natures, we are masters ourselves and are starting to realize this. This is what one master meant when he answered the question "How does one become a master?" by saying "Simply let him out." From the outset we are always ourselves; fundamentally, the person we seek to become. The inner urge that sets us seeking is itself the thing we are looking for.

The outer and inner master come only when we need them, when we have reached a point in our development where separation from Being has become a source of suffering. A master is someone who has overcome this separation and reunited himself with his true nature. In our true nature we are at one with Being; in the worldly ego we are parted from it. The worldly ego separates us from the animals, but when it claims to be absolute it also separates us from God. This is why we must bring worldly ego and true nature together and make them serve Being. We can find the strength to do this in our true nature, which is permanently at one with Being. The master's task is to let this strength become conscious and effective.

The anguish of looking for the master is the anguish of losing one's way—the Way we are now seeking. We have already seen that the master is an inner as well as an outer authority and that the way we are looking for is also within us to start with. True nature is Being present within us, and we must not see it as a static image but as the inborn way on which our task is gradually to achieve a form that fuses true nature with the ego and makes it effective in the world—that is, capable of transforming existence in and around us in a manner consonant with Being.

The inner master is primal knowledge, now active and transforming us from within, of the inborn way on which we can fulfill our destiny. He appears when this knowledge combines with an ethical imperative—a new conscience that has power to generate the way on which Life can reveal itself ever more fully and clearly in the world. And so the master is also the voice of absolute conscience, something very different from conscience as the voice of a given community's standards and expectations.

The inner master is awareness of our own potential, of the person we could and should be. We sense, recognize, and obey the inner master (this potential) only when we reach a certain stage in our development. We do not hear his summons until we are in some sense ready to follow it—and following it requires not just courage but a certain humility as well.

There is nothing arrogant about recognizing the master in ourselves. This recognition is at once inspiration, happiness, and burden. Following the way that now opens in front of us is a weighty task, and to shoulder that weight we need humility. To be truly humble is not just to avoid seeming more than one is—it is also to accept that one is, in some respects, more than one seems. There exists a false modesty, actually a disguised fear of greater responsibility, that prevents the inner master from emerging. We have independent power to find and follow the Way, but this power becomes effective only when we sense the inner master as an instinctive urge to "be like God" and accept that urge. If we say that certain people have missed their way, we are implying that they could in fact have followed it.

There is an inner master, and there is an inner student.

Master—student—Way: these three belong inextricably together, not only in the world but in ourselves as well. When the inner master wakes, the inner student wakes with him; and both exist only in relation to the inner Way, on which the master leads and the student follows—not only outwardly but inwardly, too. To recognize and accept an outer master, one must first wake to the inner master, wake with him to the inner student, and wake in both to the inner Way.

The Here-and-now Master

Whenever it is used of a specific person living in a specific place and time, the word *master* denotes someone in whom Life is fully, actively, and physically present in human shape. In the master, Life comes to awareness of itself as lived actuality, is released into creative freedom, is empowered to guide and create, and is liberated into irresistible change. The here-and-now master is one of the ultimate forms of humanity, transcending the ordinarily human.

Marked by and charged with this greater Life, guided by and serving it, the master has matured to a point where he can manifest the Absolute. He has overcome many of the obstacles that prevent Life from emerging fully, and is thus human and superhuman at the same time. His ways of thinking and acting are no longer ruled by the world's social, moral, or theological systems and demands; for he is rooted in otherworldly freedom. He may respect the world's conventions, but is not obliged to conform to them. This is what makes him a troublemaker. Life's truth accepts the world's fixities only as long as they neither interfere with nor obstruct the process of becoming.

The master's broadened consciousness provides a sounding board on which the ground notes of Being can ring out in all their purity. He is also a perfect medium, and through him these ground notes can ring out and reecho in others as well.

The way in which Life's unity is present in the master's consciousness is not the way in which it is present in pre-mental consciousness before it loses its own unity and becomes fragmented. The unity active in the master is also light-years away from the womblike, primitive unity that sucks so many people back into the warm, protective grasp of an inchoate "oneness" and stifles their individuality for good. What the master embodies is unity refound—a unity preceded by death and dislocation of the original unity. Being's presence in his consciousness is the sequel to catastrophe—loss of union with Being, and the brutal tearing out of the primal roots. The master's light is born of the night through which he has passed, and his knowledge harks back to a time when everything he knew had been lost. He is strong because he knows all about weakness and death, and can love because he has known and endured the anguish of solitude.

It is not only because he embodies what the student is seeking and senses in him that the master can reach the student. Often, the reverberation of the master's past estrangement from Being goes even further toward bridging the gap, allowing him to draw close to the student in his or her anguish, as if they were still united by some fraternal bond. This is what makes the master's love a special kind of love.

In the master, Life comes to awareness of itself in human form. Basically, the master knows that it is not he who is coming to awareness of Life, but Life that is coming to awareness of itself in him. In the master, Life senses itself in the radiance of a special experience, reveals itself in the light of a special knowledge, and becomes effective in the healing power of a very special activity.

Becoming a master is a matter of becoming a transparent medium for one's own true nature. Because he is in touch with his own true nature, the master can see the true nature in everything he meets. And because he has become a window for the Absolute, he can turn others into mediums as well. Wherever the master is, Life becomes manifest.

The master embodies the truth of Life as the supra-antithetical tension of time and eternity. His task is not to resolve this tension but to make it real and give it form—to make it palpable in terms of future possibility in such a way that it acquires creative force to transform the world and bring it into line with Being.

The master embodies Life, knows the truth, and leads on the Way that brings truth to form.

The three essential qualities of Life are all combined and present in the master. Life's fullness is tangibly apparent in his primal potency and strength. Its laws and order are manifest in the special authority that allows him to generate form that accords with Being, even when he "does" nothing. Its unity can be sensed in his primal connection with everything that lives, in the depth of his humanity, and in a love that has largely left "feeling" behind. All of these are signs of his maturity. And so he also possesses the three primal qualities of true nature: power, status, and maturity.

The master stands in the radiance of Life, present within him and infusing his consciousness. And so he stands in the light of a higher insight and in strength that has power to act and transform.

The master is the appointed intermediary between the world and otherworldly Being. He looses the ties that prevent people from attaining true selfhood and shows them what the poles are. Having done this, he again bridges the gap in a way that makes it possible for world-ego and true nature to coexist and cooperate consciously in a process of creation and redemption.

The master is master only in relation to a world that is capable of changing and wants to change. The sage requires no students, but a master without students is like music without listeners—nonexistent.*

The master is master only because he is linked to a

*Cf. Lama Anagarika Govinda, *Der Weg der Weissen Wolken* (Munich: O. W. Barth-Verlag).

higher authority, at whose command he acts and to which he is responsible. When he mediates between heaven and earth, he always acts at its bidding. He never claims to be the source himself, but refers to a higher reality, to an otherworldly authority, to God or to his own master. His submission to this authority and his veneration for those who have served it before him are an intrinsic part of what he is and does. Its presence shapes and infuses all his "ceremonial" actions.

A master who lacks humility is no master, or is an inverted master—the satanic emanation and embodiment of transcendence usurped by the ego.

The master is neither a schoolmaster nor a reading master, but—as Meister Eckhart, the fourteenth-century mystic, put it—a life-master. He is the embodiment and mediator, the guardian and champion of Life, perpetually renewing itself in everlasting movement and change. And so nothing we are, nothing we become, can satisfy him. For the student, listening to a master means handing himself over to everlasting uproar. He can only do this in the long run if he starts to hear primal silence in this tumult and also to sense it in the master, behind all his sudden changes of direction.

The stillness of Life lies beyond peace and uproar, beyond silence and noise. It expresses the peace that enters once we start seeing our own and the world's restlessness as the background and active source of ultimate tranquility.

The master's entrance is like the lion's roar—it heralds a life-and-death struggle, the struggle that no one destined for a higher level is spared, that no one called to the Way can escape. It is a struggle that holds the ultimate promise but demands the ultimate effort: "dying and becoming" in the fullest sense, and not once, but as the Way's everlasting rule and principle.

The master is not a conventionally perfect human being. He does not embody the traditional values and virtues of beauty, truth, and goodness in any obvious sense. He says and does things that horrify the normal, decent citizen—and repeatedly aims his sharpest arrows at precisely that normal, decent citizen. He does not shore things up, but turns them upside-down. No one can say what he will do next. He is as unpredictable and contradictory as life itself, for he embodies Life, and is himself life and death, Yin *and* Yang in neverending alternation. He is both a creative and a redeeming force. He is living *and* dying—perilous, incomprehensible, and hard. Peace, security, and harmony are our normal human goals, but the master tears up the roots we have barely put down, knocks over the things we thought secure, sunders the bonds we have contracted, and pulls away the ground on which we stand; for the point is walking and not standing still, traveling and not arriving, change and not completion. Life exists only as transition—and the master keeps it alive by making transition a neverending process.

The master overturns the neat and ordered. But no sooner has he done so—shattered the existing structure, created what looks like total chaos, and left his student floored and gasping—than that student suddenly senses that something new is taking shape, a new order being born and a new form emerging. And he starts to see the love behind the master's harshness and the meaning of the darkness into which the master plunged him, for a new and unexpected light is dawning.

The master's activity has its roots in inactivity. Fundamentally, he "does" nothing, but acts as a medium for Life, which works through him and transforms others in the process.

The master knows all about being a student, for being a master means having the eye that recognizes the students, the heart that loves them from true nature to true nature, and the hand that guides them both gently and sternly. The master knows about the Way—and about the things in people that prevent them from following it. He knows about the conditions that allow them to act as mediums, or stop them from doing so. He knows about the steps that mark the way written into the student's true nature, and helps the student to take them. He knows about the laws of becoming, and the various levels on the path. He knows about the guiding lights on the Way—and also about the will-o'-the-wisps that lead the student astray. He knows about the kind of dying we must do before we can wake to new life.

Students

The eternal master is Life on the way to worldly manifestation of itself in human shape. The here-and-now master appears only in a person who is recognized as bearing witness to Life by another person who summons and needs him.

Whenever people previously content with ego-world consciousness come to see that they are in fact the prisoners of contingency, the moment of total change has come. When they then unmistakably hear the voice of the Absolute in their true nature, hear the summons to conversion, and wake to the possibility of obeying it, the student wakes within them. But they become students in the full sense only when they *decide* to accept the "great service" and call for a master to guide them.

People can be said to have woken and become students only when the other dimension calls them in a way that casts doubt on the whole direction in which they were previously heading—in other words, when they receive the certainty, or at least the commanding intuition, of a Life that is no longer worldly but remains transcendent through every aspect of worldly life and action. When the student wakes, the inner master wakes with him—and the instant, urgent search for a real-life, here-and-now master itself guarantees that such a master will shortly make his appearance.

Students and masters are parts of the same process. They are twin aspects of Life, breaking through to self-manifestation in the world, both in the consciousness of one individual and in the encounter of two. Fundamentally, we are all students—if only dormant students—of the everlasting master, potential disciples of Being, which is present in our true nature and calling us to follow it.

The only way in which we can fulfill our destiny is by attending to the inner master. This means that every one of us is naturally a potential student—an inner student corresponding to the inner master. And just as the master has always been within us, so the student, too, has always been there. That student's destiny is to accompany the archetypal master as the archetypal student—that is, the archetype of the man or woman prepared to follow unquestioningly on the way that leads to union with Being.

It is not always some great, cataclysmic event that wakes a person and turns him or her into a student. The slightest thing can suddenly provoke the inner change; for waking to studenthood has always been prepared for a long time beforehand by the anguish of true nature struggling to breathe. The change can express itself in many different ways, ranging from physical discomfort through neurosis to deep depression and suicidal urges. The greater the anguish caused by the suppression of true nature the greater the likelihood that some pinprick will trigger the change—some trivial incident that suddenly makes true nature ring out, unexpectedly eveals the hidden and unknown, and "initiates" the seeker, throwing open the door to the mystery and bringing something "totally different" palpably home. When this happens to us, we are touched by the great unknown and, for an instant, are utterly confused. At once enraptured and appalled, we taste—if only for a split second—an entirely new kind of freedom. We may feel gripped by some wholly new power and a part of it. We sense another dimension, an unknown fullness and depth, and in all of it the promise of a life that was previously not possible. But the whole thing must not simply rush by and evaporate in a burst of joy: it must be experienced as a summons and obligation if we are to wake and become students. To see the light, it is not enough merely to be shown it.

This first initiation experience of an outside element breaking into natural, worldly consciousness wakes us in this sense only if we understand what it demands of us—an effort wholly different in nature and purpose from anything we have ever been asked to do or not do before.

This first experience also opens up possibilities that make the whole of our previous existence seem blind, deaf, shallow, meaningless, and lonely. Suddenly a new possibility is offered, something that depends on inner change and not, like everything in our past life, on visibly doing well in a worldly sense. As new students, we are filled with a new happiness and a new sense of obligation because the law we must follow from now on is an inner, not an outer, one— indeed, we ourselves in our true nature are the law, and obeying it depends on ourselves and not on outside circumstances.

We wake to studenthood when we not only hear the summons from an old reality to a new one but are ready to obey it simply because we sense that the way to which it calls us is both the only way and the way we were personally meant to follow. We must travel it without knowing it, as if we had grasped the truth of the old Indian saying "Not knowing the way, I move forward on the way, with hands outstretched, with hands outstretched."

But when can a person call himself a student? He can call himself a student "only when he is consumed with longing, when anguish has brought him to the ultimate barrier and he feels that he must break through it or die.

"He can call himself a student only when restlessness of heart holds him fast and will not let him go until he finds a way of stilling it.

"He can call himself a student only when he has set foot

on the way, knows that he cannot turn back, and is willing to be led forward and obey.

"He can call himself a student only when he is capable of unquestioning faith, can follow without understanding, and is ready to face and endure any trial.

"He can call himself a student only when he can be hard with himself and is prepared to leave everything for the sake of the One that is forcing its way within him toward the light.

"It is only when the unconditional has seized him that he can accept every condition and endure all the hardships of the way on which the master leads him.

"ALL OR NOTHING is written in large characters above the door through which the student passes on his way to the exercise room. He must leave everything behind, but can take one certainty with him: it is not caprice that awaits him, but the clearsighted wisdom of the master, who focuses unwaveringly on what he really is and spares no effort to bring it to life; a kind of dying is expected of him, but its meaning is not death, but Life beyond life and death; not the destruction of existence, but Being that irradiates it."*

When the student is born, the inner master is born too. Although he cannot know the meaning of the term *master,* the new student still intuits it; for the master within has woken in the form of a new conscience. This conscience is mandatory primal knowledge of the innate way in our true nature that leads to total change and perfects us as mediums for Being. It has nothing in common with primitive conscience, which is simply a fear of punishment and operates only when punishment seems imminent. Similarly, absolute conscience has nothing in common with the voice of worldly obligation—the voice with which people, projects, or communities speak when we disobey their rules and which embodies the principle "What the whole is determines how the parts behave." The

*Karlfried Graf Dürckheim, *Zen and Us,* trans. Vincent Nash (New York: E. P. Dutton, 1987), pp. 76–77.

inner master's voice demands only that we be totally faithful to the inner core experienced in our own soul, and it may even tell us to reject all our worldly ties and obligations. This is why absolute conscience can also make someone who has genuinely woken to studenthood capable of actions that the world mistakenly condemns as faithless, cruel, or treacherous.

The omnipresence of the Absolute expresses itself as absolute conscience in the person who has woken to studenthood. The inner master's voice is uncompromising, and no one can call himself a student unless he is willing to obey it. This obedience also implies unconditional discipline.

There are two types of discipline—imposed and accepted. Imposed discipline means subjection to an outside authority which is experienced as an alien force and a limitation on freedom. Accepted discipline expresses fidelity to a personal decision concerning our true nature—the source of all true freedom.

In accepted discipline, we trade freedom of the ego (freedom to do or not do whatever the ego wants) for freedom from the ego (freedom to do what our true nature wants). Here, we ourselves are, as the inner master in our own true nature, the guiding authority. Even contact with the outer master serves only as a repeated, revitalizing spur to the inner master. If there is no inner master, the outer master has no power to transform—indeed, there are no masters. This is also why a genuine master repeatedly withdraws, leaving the student to himself. In doing this, he is testing and summoning the inner master—and making way for him.

Master and student share the same living space and breathe the same air—air that has a numinous quality and blows from another world: stimulating and refreshing, challenging and reassuring, nurturing and nourishing, mysterious and comforting all at the same time.

Master and student are bathed in the same light—the light that turns everything into a window for true nature.

Master and student share the same warmth—the

warmth of unbroken contact from true nature to true nature, linking them both to each other and to all the world besides.

Master and student share the same energy of Life flooding through them, sustaining them, giving them wings, and driving them on. They also serve the same master—divine Being, forcing its way on toward manifestation of itself.

When we wake to studenthood we are caught between two fires—the master (both inner and outer), who wants to make us witness utterly to divine Being, and the worldly self that is still selfishly (or even selflessly and objectively) focused on the world and has yet to find its true center. This tension is not the same thing as the unconscious tension between ego and true nature. As new students we are aware of our true nature's demands and of the tension between these and the world's demands. This is something more than the growing, unconscious anguish that we feel when we force ourselves to ignore true nature's promise and loyally play the world's game. To progress as students on the way we must, for a time and repeatedly, submit entirely to our own true nature and thus endure the world's anger at our betrayal of it. Only when we have succeeded in sensing true nature outside the worldly element will we be able to find it again within the worldly element and continue to serve it in all our worldly doings.

A person who has woken to studenthood is moving toward new human status—the status of being on the way to the Way. Waking to studenthood is not a single step but a multistage process. It begins when the inner call is experienced, listened to, and first obeyed. This marks the entry to the Way. A distinction must therefore be drawn between two stages: waking to the possibility and waking to the actuality of studenthood.

An Eastern master was once asked to define the difference between students and masters, and answered: "When a person can really call himself a student, he's already where the master is—on the Way—only you can see it more clearly in the master's case." This means that people who have really

47

become students are no longer in danger, in their constant battles with the worldly ego, of betraying the neverending process of change that leads to manifestation of the Absolute—that is, of rebelling against the master. Those, on the other hand, who have merely opened their eyes to the possibility of studenthood are still a doubtful quantity. It is true that the Absolute has already touched them, that they are willing to follow and may even have promised to perform the first exercises—but they are still not totally committed to the Way. They are on the way to the Way, but have not yet passed through the gate of total change, beyond which there is no turning back. Take the eternal prayer as a benchmark: we can say that students have passed through the gate when they no longer utter the prayer but when the prayer utters them. They remain human, of course, and are thus repeatedly tempted to stand still, but the real danger is past. To say that *they* are on the Way in this sense is really to say that the Way has got them—and will keep them.

Even potential students are already novices in the secret order. They make the grade not simply by hearing the voice of Being, the call of the Absolute, but by actually moving in the "direction" of the call. At this point, the uncomplicated unity of the world, the unity experienced by the natural self, falls apart. The old worldview based on our five senses; our rational powers; our awareness of truth, beauty, and goodness; our ethical notions of achievement and good conduct and a smattering of "religion" not only becomes too narrow (like a building that needs another story); its foundations and its whole design are suddenly wrong, rather as if we were birds, had found we could fly, and suddenly saw the cage that seemed a refuge for what it really was: a prison! If laziness or fear keeps us in prison all the same, then we are betraying our true nature.

People touched by Being are facing a totally new challenge, are radiantly, gloriously bathed in a new light. Quite simply, they know that a wholly new reality has emerged within, or more accurately, that they have emerged to a new reality, or more accurately still, that they have genuinely emerged as a wholly different person from the person they had previously supposed themselves to be. But to become this person in and for the world as well, they need a master.

What the Master Does—How He Does It

The master has five ways of doing what he does: doctrine, commands, charisma, example, shock tactics.

Doctrine

The medieval scholastics had a saying: "Philosophy is the handmaid of theology." In other words, theology—meaning here faith anchored in consciousness—comes first. It is not founded on discursive thought, but directly revealed. However, we are thinking beings, and thus have a natural need and duty to go as far as we can in raising the nonrational beliefs of subjective consciousness to objective consciousness as well, interpreting them rationally, grasping them conceptually, and fitting them into systems.

This is why the truth of belief has always been accompanied by doctrine. The same applies to the truth of Life, which fulfills itself in and through the master and which the master has the task of communicating. It is true that what is really at stake in the master-student relationship cannot be explained and conceptualized but can only leap from heart to heart—but it is equally true that words and "doctrine" are essential components and accompaniments of the guidance provided by the master.

The necessity of doctrine is felt all the more keenly when the master is dealing with intelligent students who are not content merely to imitate and obey but want to think things through with him. The more accustomed students are to ordering their lives rationally or the more they aspire to do so (that is, the more they try to clarify the knowable in concepts), the more they expect to find what the master gives them grounded in a worldview that is something more than an ideology or wishful thinking. It must be founded on experience and embody knowledge that is also conceptually convincing and conceptually tenable. The heart of the master's teaching cannot be communicated intellectually, but the ways in which it comes to awareness, and the preconditions and consequences of its doing so, can be raised to conceptual consciousness for the thinking person.

True religious feeling can be understood only as the expression of a direct link back to the Absolute, and the Absolute touches us only in experiences that cannot, ultimately, be conveyed in words. But we still have a need to investigate the starting point, meaning, and stages of the process of change that starts with these experiences and leads back to them, and to understand its psychological basis and effects sufficiently for its meaning to withstand objective inquiry as well.

A true master's doctrine satisfies the need to understand in two ways. First, it demonstrates the validity of specific things he has said by showing how they are anchored in the overall pattern of movement and change that makes up the way he points out. Second, it strengthens and justifies the student's hope that he will receive the help he needs to "become himself from his true nature." It thus answers both a rational and an existential question.

The masters' legacies are not philosophical systems. However much or however little they may have said or written, the purpose of it all is merely to get "the central point" across. Masters always have one thing only to communicate. But the one, repeated message always sounds new, and the devices they use to convey it, the means they choose to illuminate it, and the paths on which they lead their students to the Way are infinitely varied.

A master may follow the example of countless masters before him in presenting his doctrine—may, for example, use formulas derived from a venerable tradition. But the way in which he passes it on is always *his own*—is the way in which it lives in *him*. Individual witness is the only way of communicating the universal. Even when he relies word for word on traditional formulas, he conveys their meaning in his own way, giving the hearer the impression that something which has, perhaps, been said a thousand times before is now flowing directly, for the first time, from the fountainhead of life. The master's teaching may also interpret a tradition in its own way, may resemble a homemade metaphysic—the decisive element is always the spark that leaps the gap. It is not what he says that matters so much, but the way that he says it—and the fact that *he* is saying it. For what is said takes effect only if the person saying it is himself what he says. It is not what the master says, but what he is, that convinces.

And so, formal instruction is not the central part of the process. The thing that really counts is heart-to-heart communication, communication from true nature to true nature—from Being, which the master is in his true nature, to Being, which the student also is in his true nature.

The master "does not behave like a teacher. He does not probe, correct, or advise. He is filled with the One, and focuses solely on the One. He looks only at what his student really is, feels his way toward it from what he really is himself, loves it, tries to make contact with it, and drives unwaveringly forward in search of it. For him, everything that blocks the student's true nature is summed up in one fatal error: a clinging to things that the student regards as unchanging and that stop him from changing himself. This is the root of the evil, and it must be torn out completely. Everything the master says and does thus bursts spontaneously and directly from the realm of the 'undetermined' and sets out to liberate the undetermined in his students too. This is a matter of instant, here-and-now contact, for this is the only type of contact that reflects the everlasting *now* and in which the student can receive the lightning-stroke of revelation, smashing through the system that has so far held him prisoner. Every familiar image, every well-worn concept, every merely conventional description of evil is dangerous. Only speech or silence, action or inaction, which comes here and now, once and unrepeatably, from the heart—from direct contact with the One—can get through to the student, touch on the presence of Being within him, wake it, and bring it to the light."*

Every tradition of masters exists on two levels: first, as a complex of stories, images, and concepts that natural reason can grasp, because they are aimed at the natural ego, but that easily petrify and lose their vital substance when interpreted "comprehensibly" (the danger that every religion faces in its "popular" traditional form); and second, as the esoteric meaning of those stories and images—their inner core, which concepts cannot seize. This is the deeper meaning of the symbols, and only those "with ears to hear" can catch it—the intangible center of the whole, which also gleams through the popular forms and touches the believer in them, but is truly revealed only to a higher consciousness. Only someone who is ready—who has ears to hear—can catch the secret meaning of the master's teaching in all the images, and catch it in a way that repeatedly touches and binds him anew, even to silence!

As soon as certain stories and images take root in the student's mind, as soon as certain formulas and concepts acquire independent validity and substitute imperceptibly for the living truth, the master sets out to destroy them. Images and concepts must never be anything more than pointers, reminders, hopeful indications of a possible experience. "The finger pointing at the moon must not be confused with the moon," say the Eastern masters.

*Dürckheim, *Zen and Us*, pp. 77–78.

One of the signs that a student has "understood," has really woken to the truth, has traditionally been rejection of the words in which the truth was first communicated to him or her. Again and again, students have burned the sacred books of doctrine, for written words are "empty straw" compared with the new life within them. If the master is a real master, this action—which shocks others—delights him.

At the same time, sacred scripture has always played a very special role. Personally transmitted by master to student, it can become, in an immediate sense, the Absolute's gift of itself to the seeker—the presence of the Divine. This is why people traditionally touch it when swearing an oath, why it has a special place in the home, and why it is treated with special veneration. Other objects, too, can carry the supernatural energy of the master who bestows them, can embody the living and effective presence of his teaching. If we try to explain the living significance of sacred objects in psychological terms, we are forgetting that human beings are living subjects to whom the world is real only when it means something to them personally, and "deep" only when they respond to it deeply—and are able to open themselves to it.

A master can sum up and convey the heart of the living message in a single image, event, gesture, or even word. His function here is a priestly one, and this is particularly clear when he touches students, sets a sacred sign on their forehead, or gives them a sacred word on their way—only one syllable, perhaps, but a syllable that makes the Divine itself a presence when the student repeats it.

Students who imagine they can start by discarding intellection altogether are seriously mistaken. If they ask why they should bother to go the way of thought when they know from the start that it leads to a dead end, the master tells them: "Because to think is human!" Thinking may indeed be a mere shadow of the direct perception that ultimately matters when nothing else does; but on the inner way no one can jump over his or her own shadow. The positive must be found through the negative, the right way through the wrong one, unity through division, Life through death. We must uncover, accept, and come to terms with our shadow (what we naturally are and try to forget) or it will leap up behind us when we least expect it—usually when we think we are well forward on the way—trip us by the heels, and bring us crashing, forcing us to start again from the beginning. This is why people who have already gone as far as reason will take them are likeliest, in our own day, to see and recognize Being, which reason cannot grasp, and to register the qualities in which it first speaks to us.

Dismissing or at least distrusting "doctrine" (systematic, conceptual knowledge of the meaning and process of change) is rooted in the fear that reality reflected may take the place of reality lived. The golden rule of all true pastoral care is to avoid "helpful" concepts, which merely irritate seekers without really giving them anything. This is why the mystics have always been wary of concepts, because concepts wipe experience out by pinning it down. We are told that a student, who had been enlightened, once answered "Yes" when his master asked him jovially, "And so, now you have it?" and that this was enough to make the master roar "You have nothing!" and turn him out—simply because his affirmative reply had pinned something down. But concepts that explain and define, that kill the living heart of living words and deeds, are not the only ones. There are also concepts that point to and preserve experience—but only those who "understand" (have experienced Being) know what they mean. Systematic progress on the path of expanding consciousness is impossible without such concepts.

Commands

The difference between masters and conventional psychotherapists is that the master interferes, leads, corrects, and issues instructions. And the difference between the student and the conventional subject of psychotherapy is that the student expects these instructions and is willing—indeed eager—to follow them. The difference becomes particularly plain when the master tests his students' confidence, which is the very basis and justification of the whole relationship, by telling them to do things they do not understand and do not want to do.

A modern young man or woman who knew nothing of the master's meaning or purpose, would write this off at once as typical patriarchal tyranny. Indisputably, the time has come for certain kinds of paternal authority to disappear ("Why should I?"—"Because I say so!" Or "I don't know why you children keep harping on about freedom—in my house, anyone can do what he wants!"). It is undoubtedly important to stress and encourage independence from the start, to recognize that children also have their human dignity and to see that it is respected. The master's authority, however, is grounded in the fact that his orders follow the law of the student's own true nature, which he has the task of helping to develop.

Authority always derives from the fact that the person giving orders embodies more fully than the person obeying them the system that the latter has agreed to serve. Obedience thus expresses the whole that is active in both. Here again, what the whole is determines how the parts behave; and this applies to the superior—schoolteacher, boss, officer, abbot, or master—as much as it does to the subordinate. A significant point on the subordinate's side is, of course, whether orders are obeyed out of choice or compulsion—in other words, whether he has opted for the relationship or has been forced into it. Another is whether the subordinate's original decision is still personally valid. On the superior's side, the relationship's validity depends on whether he genuinely represents the whole that he officially embodies—on whether the master genuinely and convincingly represents the Life he stands for.

In every genuine master-student relationship, the student always remains free, and this freedom is expressed in obedience. The discipline that he accepts is not external, but internal. Just as he is free to choose one master rather than another, so he is free to move on whenever he wants to—because he feels that he no longer needs a master, because he no longer feels equal to the Way's demands, or because he wants to change masters. This is one of the saddest things that masters have to face—repeatedly being left, for various reasons, by students on whom they have worked wholeheartedly for years. When students want to leave, no one tries to stop them. But while they remain, they accept the master's authority freely. Indeed, students are quicker to complain that their master is not testing them enough, is not being sufficiently demanding, than that he is being unduly hard on them. Everything depends, however, on their knowing that the Way is an ongoing battle with the puny, self-willed ego, whose only concern is its own security. They follow the master's instructions even when this is hard—not in blind obedience to a stronger worldly will, but because the master *knows* and *is* more than they know and are and can help them throw off the ego's tyranny and enter the freedom of true nature.

The existential relationship between one true nature and another is the context of everything a master tells his student. This kind of relationship always points to primal unity. For this reason, a master's teaching does not merely derive power from the fullness of Being present within him, or find justification in the laws of Being, which he embodies and transmits—it also reflects the unity of Being that binds him to the student. Indeed, his hardest, most perplexing instructions are rooted in his love of the student. They spring from unity working within him as task and obligation—unity with the student's true nature, which is destined to realize itself in the world through the process of change that the master unleashes and demands. The deeper the existential links, the more carelessly the master appears to treat his students, even giving them indications and instructions that defy the power of natural reason—but are actually signs of his untiring preparedness, imagination, and courage. The presence of the other dimension justifies it all.

Practice invariably occupies a central place in the master's instructions. Exercise is always a vital element on the way of initiation. The master tells his students which exercises to do, shows them how to set about it, monitors their performance, knows what the stages are, and recognizes the signs of progress—particularly when technique is no longer the point and the signs stop showing that the ego, which is still determined to "succeed," is interfering, and start showing that true nature is beginning to enter the student's consciousness. In short, the master follows each step in the process of change furthered by the exercise. He chooses the exercise and decides how often and how intensively the student should do it. Many of the exercises used on the way of initiation try the student's natural powers to the ultimate limit of exhaustion, but if his or her general attitude is right they also summon the supernatural for the first time. It is only when the ego gives up and gives way—provided that the student's real center does not falter—that the new world beyond the ego's horizon can appear.

When his students exercise, a master must keep their overall attitude right by endlessly repeating the same instructions and exhortations. This applies not only to specific exercises but also to their general posture. The master instantly catches the slightest departure from right posture, the faintest false note in the voice, the most fleeting sign of complacency, every shadow of untruth, every flicker of pretense. And he swoops to correct it. With praise, however, he is sparing.

Charisma

The master also works through charisma, radiating and communicating something that has nothing to do with words and actions. Indeed, this wordless something is the vital element in everything he says and does—and it works in many ways.

For one thing, it confers a special strength. Of course, the master reduces the clamorous ego to nothing, and this makes the student feel small; but the master also releases true nature's energy, which the ego normally obscures, and this is why the student may also sense, with the master (and, even more, on leaving him), a new strength. In the master's presence, extinction can also be looked calmly in the face—as if everything that could be destroyed had simply melted away and only the indestructible was left.

The light that shines in the master's charisma pierces the fog of ready-made certainties, frees the student from it, and unleashes a new creative energy. It mercilessly smashes through untruth and grinds it to atoms. Like the strength the master gives his students, it comes from another dimension—as if from an infinitely distant source. But because the master is a perfect medium it can flow through him into the world.

When the master is present, the truth comes to light. Questions answer themselves before they are uttered. Obscurities vanish and façades collapse.

In the master's light, the indwelling law reveals itself and becomes active as knowledge and as conscience. In the master's radiance, the form that matches Being takes on outline. False form is sensed and cannot be preserved, and true form emerges.

The master's charisma is hard and demanding, but also full of warmth. It gives his students a sense of oneness with their true nature and releases them from ties that are foreign to it. The master's love aims at union with the otherworldly; it liberates from worldly ties. This is precisely what gives his charisma its power for those who are called to the Way—it is not just liberating and satisfying, but also dangerous and exciting. It is like the cold plunge that seems to stop the heart and then sets it beating faster. This is what makes the master's love special—it saves by destroying.

And so the master operates as strength, light, and love, without doing anything—simply from the radiance that is always the sign that Being has seized a person and is acting in and through him.

Example

If he has to, a master is ready to violate a given community's code—but he never violates the law by which it really lives. Sometimes, however, he can obey this law only by turning the community's tidy systems upside-down. This is why he is never a model of civic virtue—never an example for the upright citizen to follow.

A master is always one of a kind, someone who cannot and should not be imitated. He is always an original—a unique, individual medium—bearing witness to something of universal human value in an individual form.

Every human being can follow the law that applies to us all in just one way—his or her own. An Eastern master was once asked how he could talk so much about individuality when he saw the All-One as the only reality, the only thing that mattered, and immediately answered: "Because they're the same thing!" Each true nature can express the All-One only in its own way. We cannot experience the divine by shutting our individuality out—but only by admitting and accepting it.

A master serves the cause of Life only by leading his students to themselves and bringing out the originality in them. This is the difference between real masters, who make their students independent, even allowing them to say what they like, and pseudo-masters, who usually insist on being imitated and stifle their students' individuality by forcing them to parrot certain fixed formulas.

For the student, the master represents the looked-for, longed-for, ideal reality in human shape. He embodies it in his words and behavior—and, even more, simply in what he is. But his example is interpreted correctly only if it wakes the inner master and, through the inner master, the student's real self.

The turning point in a student's life often comes when he or she first meets the master. At this first meeting, "it" comes home to the student for the first time; and the impact increases as time goes on. The first encounter lights the fire, and the master's continuing presence feeds it.

The fruitfulness of the student's relationship with the master is clear in the aftereffects of every meeting. However startling, crushing, or perilous the encounter may have been, the student feels a new sense of joy and liberation afterward.

The master acts most clearly as model and exemplar when he uses a skill to make his point. When he does, his skill is matchless—indeed, it must be perfect. But when he is leading his students on the way to the Way—when his skill is an exercise leading to the Way—the exemplary significance is not in the skill itself but in the human qualities behind it and, ultimately, in the superhuman force that spectators sense beyond both.

This fact—that, ultimately, it is the supra-worldly that speaks through what the master does—becomes particularly clear when the master himself barely retains the physical strength to give proof of his skill. At this point, the way in which he goes to work and takes up his instrument (for example, the bow that he can scarcely draw) may itself be enough— the spark jumps and the spectators "see," even if the arrow falls short.

The master of a skill has purged his technique of ego and is able to hand it over to a higher power and let that power act for him. No ordinary yardstick can be used to measure the result, since something more than visible achievement is at stake—namely, revelation of another dimension. When the student finally achieves mastery, this dimension reveals itself in five ways:

In the basic attitude of the person performing the feat.
In the perfection of the feat itself.
In the power reflected in the feat.
In what the person performing it experiences.
In its numinous effect on those who witness it.

The master performs the feat, not because he is more skillful than the student, but because he *is* more, and because this means that his skill is fearlessly, selflessly, carelessly at his command. And it is this, and not his greater skill, that makes him an example to his students on the Way of initiation. He manifests the Absolute, not just in his special feats, but in everything he does, and indeed simply in his way of "being there." It is the Absolute sounding through his physical presence that makes him a master.

The master is a model because he is a window to his own true nature. In everything he says or does, he is, quite simply, himself. His actions express what he is, naturally and with none of the conventional ego's restraints. To this extent, he is also beyond ordinary conceptions of virtue.

When a master is labeled as good, devoted, self-sacrificing, gentle, and loving, or, on the contrary, as wildly egocentric, self-willed, irascible, aloof, and harsh to the point of cruelty, the description may be true or false. Either way, it has nothing to do with what he is as a master or the things that make him a master. His way of living his own life is determined by the way in which Life comes to form in him; he himself is marked, molded, and energized by it, and never stops to wonder how this affects others. He has outrun the standards of the worldly ego, with its roots in community, and is bound only to Life. Others' reactions are as irrelevant as his own compliance or noncompliance with their social codes. The inner truth drives him to tear down the ornamental façades that surround him. Here, however, lies the temptation for false masters.

Sauce for the goose is not necessarily sauce for the

gander. There are many who usurp and distort the master's right to obedience, all the way down to certain faith healers and fairground illusionists, false masters who ape real masters and use their privileges to make exaggerated, greedy, or morally repugnant demands on their followers. These are the "masters" who expect their followers to hand over all their money, pander to their sexual appetites, pamper them with luxuries, and venerate them slavishly.

The small-scale imitator is one kind of false master. Another and more dangerous type is the person who actually possesses a master's gifts but uses them to evil ends. Such a person represents the powers of darkness. He is genuinely in contact with transcendent, otherworldly forces, and can mobilize them in himself to work apparent wonders. An ostensible master like this is really someone whose innermost core has never been purified, who has subordinated contact with the other dimension to his everyday ego and cheapened it into sorcery. He has magnetic power over others and uses it to rob them of their independence and reduce them to blind obedience. His incontrovertible power serves his ego, which usurps the place of the divine and exacts adoration, like an idol. In all of this, it is not God who is at work but the devil.

The true master possesses higher powers and suprasensual faculties—but is quicker to conceal than display them. He does not flaunt them publicly, but uses them to serve the Absolute. As the embodiment of Life, he also works wonders. But beyond good and evil as others understand them, he remains above the world and is constantly active—creating, redeeming, and transforming.

Shock Tactics

To be genuinely open and receptive to Life, we must free ourselves of all systems that pin it down. Life's natural mode is transition. Life is inimical to permanence. Life is a constant surprise. So is the master—one never knows what he will do next.

The door to the master's reality is a narrow one. If we want to pass through it, we must discard everything that sustains us in our ordinary lives—everything that props us up and makes us feel safe, everything we know, trust, and rely on. The master questions all of this—everything we "lean on" in our daily lives. There is nothing he will not do to "subvert the objective ego and its values and, by doing so, to pull from underneath our feet the ground that prevents us from making contact with the true ground of existence. . . . If anything is fixed, it must be overthrown. If we lay claim to anything, that claim is rejected. If we cling to anything, it is torn from us. If we are proud of anything, it is held up to ridicule. Our illusions regarding ourselves are stripped bare. When we think we know something, it is made to seem absurd. And there are no lengths—no lengths whatsoever—to which a master will not go. He says and does things that we cannot begin to understand until we have grasped the lofty purpose that justifies it all: the senseless answer, the sudden onslaught, the well-aimed blow, the jarring shock, the punch in the face, the thump on the ear, the grating insult, the mocking laugh, the terrifying scream, the things that the ego cannot accept and yet must accept, the things that make the gorge rise and yet must be swallowed, the things that take us by surprise and knock us sideways, demolishing everything on which our normal picture of the world and ourselves has taught us to rely for support, uplift, and security. It is precisely when the ground is pulled away and we plummet that we may suddenly sense a truth outside our normal way of seeing, and realize that the fixed values that used to be the whole story and formerly defined our own position are simply the objective correlative of a subjective stance that our own finite understanding has determined, and that has therefore cut us off from something that can never be determined."*

*Dürckheim, *Zen and Us*, pp. 75–76.

63

"If the foundations we stand on in natural consciousness actually prevent us from experiencing Being, then the master who wants to lead us to that experience must first do everything he can to knock them away. That is why his actions often startle like bolts from the blue, why he speaks in riddles, why shock tactics are his tenderness and nonsense his logic."*

Life and the Individual

Our conventional picture of the man-God relationship is one in which God is the All-Powerful, whom we must obey, on whom we can call in times of trouble, the only one through whom we can ultimately find happiness, security, and peace. We need God to escape despair, endure the world's cruelty, and at last overcome our fear of both death and life.

God is the transcendent power that rules us, rewards or destroys us, shows itself to us or conceals itself from us, speaks to us or inflicts its silence on us. In short, we are utterly dependent on God. But we see the man-God relationship exclusively in these terms at only one stage in our development—the stage where everything that natural experience and understanding cannot reach is projected into an external, transcendent sphere that has both light and dark sides but has, at any rate, unlimited power over us. This way of seeing changes, however, when a special experience shows us that the things we cannot normally grasp are not necessarily "outside" but are within us; that, indeed, they are our real center, our true nature. This realization opens the way to a new conception of the relationship between the individual and divine Being.

When we come to see the Absolute as divine Being

*Ibid., p. 84.

active in our own true nature and seeking to manifest itself in and through us, we necessarily stop seeing our dependence on God as one-sided and realize that, if we depend on God, divine energy also depends on us and on our willingness to *let* it work in and through us. The turning point may come when we suddenly sense that we are actually stopping that from happening, and realize both what we are in our true nature and what we would like our true nature to make us. This insight, when it comes as something felt, and not merely thought, is a shattering one—the realization that we, as solitary individuals, can obstruct the power of Life!

We may also come to see that it is not we who are breathing, but Life that is breathing through us, and that we usually fail to let it breathe in the right way—indeed, that ingrained resistances, for which we are partly to blame, can check its flow. Similarly, we may come to see that we are ourselves preventing our true nature from taking on the form it wants to assume in us.

The depth of the impression that this realization makes on us and the depth of our conviction that we must act on it both depend on the extent to which we have already been genuinely in touch with Being and have experienced Life as the basis and meaning of all becoming and existing. The realization that we can stop Life from manifesting itself in us and in our world has the right effect on us only if we *feel* it in the deepest personal sense. It must hit us like a thunderbolt, and if it does, it may generate a new conscience.

It sounds at first totally incredible, yet it is perfectly true: Life's success in realizing its transcendent potential in the human world depends on individual human beings. This is why we can truly say, not simply that people need God, but also that God needs people. The individual must be prepared, for he is not simply seeking God: God is seeking him, too— and he must let himself be found. It is true that human life fulfills itself in fusing with the superhuman, but it is also true that Being fulfills itself in the human world only when a person lets it in—in other words, allows his or her otherworldly true nature to "become flesh."

In every flower an absolute image is struggling toward form in the contingent world of earth, water, and light. The same is true of every human being. The gardener cannot change the living image enfolded in the bud, but he can and must provide the conditions that allow it to flower and take on form. In the same way, everyone has a duty to the living image embedded in his or her true nature, the only difference being that external factors are not the only ones that prevent it from coming to form or help it to do so. The flower cannot be blamed for going wrong, but a human being can—to the extent that the process is determined by internal, as well as external, factors. If we do not become the person we were meant to be, we can blame outside causes only to a limited extent. We cannot shift all the responsibility for our own failure to live up to our true nature (that is, the mode in which Life is striving to become real in us) onto circumstances or other people. The extent to which the image within us realizes itself in this world, and the way in which it does so, is partly determined by ourselves. And, *if* we wake to our true nature, it is the "inner voice," the voice of Life—the voice of the master in ourselves—that tells us that this responsibility exists and how great it is.

All life demonstrates the same recurrent, primal happening. Being's undivided plenitude becomes differentiated, develops polar tension, breaks apart, resolves itself into recognizably separate elements, and confronts itself—without at first totally losing its original unity. However, the more the separated elements diverge, the greater the danger that they will lose contact with their roots, close themselves off in self-reliance, and lose their primal connection with Being. To a greater or lesser extent, we are all fated to succumb to this danger. The primal split occurs when the self-willed ego is born. It is caused by rational consciousness, the consciousness we use to classify in theory and "determine" in practice, shaping both ourselves and the world in the process. Ultimately,

66

our links with Being are stretched to the breaking point, and our union with it—which remains intact in our true nature—is lost in this consciousness. Opening ourselves in a new consciousness to what the old conceals from us, and what we still are in our true nature, this is the everlasting challenge. We need the master's help on the Way to meet it.

Primal entanglement with Being also carries an opposite danger—the danger of never shaking free of primal unity and so failing to achieve the independence we are meant to have. Being, the great mother, refuses to let us go. And so we are eternally pulled in two directions: between the urge toward freedom, release, and independence, and the urge that draws us back to Being as mother and protectress. To become human we have to break free of primal unity, which holds us in its womblike clasp and is constantly calling us back. But to remain human we must never entirely lose contact with this basic, sustaining, motherly force. This is one of the primal aspects of human development, and it turns up at every stage in the process. The more advanced the stage, the more acute the tension—and the greater the need to reconcile "matrix" and manly independence, worldly self-reliance with our roots in Being. This is where the person called to the Way needs a guide and mentor.

Becoming is the essence of everything that lives. The actual is both springboard and barrier to the possible. Fixtures are the enemies of Life, which is always in flux. We are all fated, however, to generate this contradiction and live it through in ourselves. The pain it causes is the only thing that enables us to hear Being and to find it. Developing as ego-world-consciousness, our consciousness is always between two fixed poles: the self-anchored ego and the world, which we also perceive as anchored and definite. The anguish we feel at the static, petrified reality of the world around us is the only thing that can open our eyes to the dynamic reality of our own true nature and to the Way we are meant to follow.

We take the first step on the path to full maturity when we realize that the ego's instinctive urge to give life "firm foundations" is actually at odds with the truth of Life, which is always on the move. This realization is not merely theoretical, not merely a source of innocent joy. It is an awakening that changes us utterly, a shock that shakes us to the core! Suddenly, the static world and systems of objective consciousness must yield to the dynamic reality of true nature that frees us and constantly makes new demands on us. Only when this happens does realization become the threshold to the way of initiation. This way does not, however, lead us to egoless, objectless, supra-worldly Being—but back to the here-and-now world and to *self*-Being, in which true nature reveals itself in a new and vitalized ego capable of bearing witness to the higher world *in* this one. At this point we are on the way to becoming masters ourselves.

We cannot play a full and responsible part in revealing the great Life within us until we have developed to a certain point, until we have clearly seen the antithesis between contingent worldly ego and absolute true nature as a threat. This recognition must come in a special experience, in which the danger is sensed as a danger to something potentially there—our true *self*, that we have the task of realizing. True nature's claim to take on form in the world must be experienced and accepted. It is only when its insistent demands win out over those of the ego and come clearly home as promise and as obligation, when their worldly realization in the true self becomes the central issue, and when we understand that we ourselves are permitted, able, and required to help realize them, that the time comes to take the great decision: to choose between serving the world in the old, self-willed way, and—still serving the world, but also transcending that service—serving Life itself. We can realize this possibility only on the Way of initiation, on which we become truly ourselves. This is a Way that we cannot travel alone. We need a guide!

The extent to which we become a self-conscious, world-conscious ego determines the extent to which, and the way in which, Life can manifest itself in us—that is, generate a form that expresses its fullness, order, and unity in an individual mode.

Whenever we can yield to Life's urge to take on form in us, we experience it as a liberating force. Whenever we resist it, we experience it as a force that destroys our own self-willed form. Whether we want to act "rightly" or actually act "wrongly" is not the decisive factor here; the only thing that counts is whether we willfully resist or give in and allow our true nature to take on form.

Our sufferings, if we obstinately resist Life's drive to become something else, are immense. The more capable we have become of understanding Life's purpose, the more fearful the suffering that our self-willed ego causes us if we still cannot accept and obey that purpose, let everything go, and make room within ourselves for the wave of Being that seeks form in us. The pain becomes even worse if we misunderstand the repeated onslaughts of Being and force ourselves to play the hero by resisting pressures that we ourselves have caused—not realizing that our own heroism (or masochism) is only prolonging the agony. The only way out is a total change of attitude. This may come when we realize that we are ourselves obstructing Life and that Life needs our cooperation and consent if it is to achieve its intended form in us.

The colors, tones, images, and forms in which cosmic "waves" and "rays" appear depend on whether and how far a given medium lets them through or resists them. This is why our own fate is always determined by the way in which we answer the Absolute's call. We realize this fully only when we reach the stage of experiencing Life in a special qualitative sense. It is seeking to manifest itself in and through us in the world, and we cannot treat it as a mere concept. It must be a qualitative experience, an experience that seizes us on the deepest level and to which we then hold fast.

Being's urge to manifest itself intensifies as we advance from stage to stage. The more the pressure builds, the closer it comes to exploding our fixed form. In this situation, we experience true nature as a destructive force—but it is destructive only when we identify entirely with our present worldly form and personality and fail to hear the master's voice. A good person can be quite as deaf to Being as a bad one, and good people often believe themselves beset by dark forces at this point. What is actually happening is that they are themselves allowing their true nature, that is trying to break through within them to the light, to turn against them. Their existing form may be noble and good, but they still have to shed it in order to follow the law of growing and becoming.

It is only at a certain stage in a person's development that Being manifests itself in truth, beauty, and goodness. They remain its medium only as long as the divine continues to touch them and honor remains a live concept, reflecting a person's willingness to die for these values and showing that he or she knows that serving them instinctively and humbly is really serving the Absolute. But these ingrained values—as soon as they generate certain fixed ways of living, thinking, and generally getting through, are naïvely accepted, and start to breed complacency—often stop Life from breaking through. And "good" people then wonder in amazement why, since they have always acted well, God is persecuting them. The reason is a simple one—their bright, tidy virtues have become a rampart; they are keeping Life out. By achieving perfect order, they have themselves turned Life into something that destroys them.

The inner master's waking means the dawning realization that everything—but everything—we do is acceptable to Life only so long as it accords with Life's will to self-manifestation. The moment it ceases to do so, Life rebels. When we are in tune with it, we sense its consent; when we are in doubt, we hear the guiding voice within.

Dialogue—listening and responding, asking questions and getting answers—is a natural part of the human condition. Experiencing ourselves in ongoing dialogue with everything we see or hear, encounter and perceive, fear or desire, is one of the distinctive features of our human consciousness. We experience everything directly as having certain "personal" features, as the outer form of an inner something that "concerns" us, speaks to us, and pleases, attracts, repels, accepts, or assails us in a definite way. We instinctively personify all the powers and forces we meet. The worlds in which we live, both inner and outer, are also registered in terms of friendly or hostile forces. And so we also naturally perceive transcendent, all-penetrating Life as an incomprehensible, mysterious, unfathomable *you*. But objective consciousness robs every experience of its vital substance; the more it encroaches, the more it threatens to reduce Life, the unfathomable, experienced *you*—whose children we are and with which we are still in primal contact—to something that has objective features and can be understood, something that reason finds less and less convincing as the first contact fades, and that eventually vanishes. It is only when growing maturity allows us to step back across the boundaries of objective consciousness to personal experience, and gives us back our ability to sense the numinous and hear the summons of the Absolute, that we stand a chance of again meeting infinite, unfathomable Being as the mighty *you* with which we have been linked from the start, of receiving its blessing and hearing its commanding voice.

The extent to which we are still in tune with Being or have moved away from it is revealed in the way the numinous affects us. It cannot get through to us while we remain cut off and imprisoned in the ego. It is only when expanding consciousness again allows us to transcend the world-ego and its way of seeing that we can meet Life again in our true nature and—in what it tells us to do and not to do, in its exhortations and instructions—experience "ourselves" simultaneously as our own master and our own everlasting student. Only when we see that we ourselves are Life in our own true nature do we grasp the nature of our "independence" and realize that we are both the servants of Life and, in our absolute origins, the intended lords of the world.

The Way

When we call the master we are calling for someone to lead us on the Way. What kind of way? The Way that opens the door to the mystery, the Way of initiation. The mystery is Life and Being hidden in our lives and existence.

The Way of initiation centers on experiencing Being and trying to achieve union with it. It has this much in common with mysticism. Like mystics, students receive the experience of Being as a gift, as grace—not something they can make happen. On the Way of initiation, however, they are constantly working, under the master's guidance, to prepare themselves for this experience; working all the time to change, attain a new human level, and become a person for whom contact with the Absolute is no longer a matter of faith, but one of its ever-deepening, all-infusing presence. Their goal on the Way of initiation is to achieve a new structure whose every shift and ripple lets the Absolute show through. The experience of the divine always remains a gift and a grace, but a person on this Way is working to achieve a state of mind and being that keeps him or her in a constant process of change—a process that is itself a sign that union with Life has been realized.

People advancing on the Way are not only increasingly conscious, in spite of all their imperfections, of their deepening links with the divine; they are also increasingly marked by the divine, and for it. For this very reason, they are increasingly, painfully conscious of everything that is still "non-divine" in themselves, so that their humility grows as they progress.

People advancing on the Way are being led. They are part of a millennial tradition. They have a master who embodies that tradition and shows them the way of transformation with its everlasting law of "dying and becoming," for a kind of dying is demanded—and not once, but repeatedly. Again and again, the same ramparts must be battered down, the same veils torn away, the same enemies defeated, and the same new kingdom conquered afresh.

The Way is a repeated breaking through to true nature, a repeated dropping of the disguises in which the adept's world-ego is reflected and on which it relies in playing its appointed worldly roles.

No one can receive the gifts of the Absolute without utterly surrendering everything that is worldly in him. There is nothing unnatural about trying to conceal our shortcomings from others, but we cannot achieve true selfhood until we let them see us as we are. Having the courage to go naked is a part of the Way.

On the Way, we accept the anguish of our own limitations and, by accepting it, repeatedly fan the spark of infinity lodged in those very limitations, recognize our true nature's law of becoming in that spark, and start living from that true nature.

The Way is the process whereby Life, which we always absolutely are in our true nature, comes to here-and-now consciousness in us and takes on form in a specific time and place. The Way is Life's way of revealing itself step by step in an individual person's individual true nature—in his or her consciousness, physical presence, and conduct.

The Way is Life's way of emerging from concealment in the human condition, where the rise of a consciousness that attempts to confine the Absolute in the contingent, to conceptualize the incomprehensible, and to pit a static reality against its dynamic, has obscured it. At the center of this consciousness stands the ego—the creator, mediator, and guardian of those fixed and permanent systems and structures that people need to live their normal lives but that also stop Life from manifesting itself in the world in otherworldly fullness, neverending change, and ultimate unity.

The Way is the process that takes people who have lost

contact with Being back, step by step, to their origin—and also forward to conscious manifestation of the Absolute within them.

The purpose of the Way is to reunite people lost in the everyday world with otherworldly Being. It requires both a master and a student, and a certain maturity. When we start on the Way, we at last become capable of fulfilling our destiny, that of bearing witness—as does the flower in its own language or the animal in its own manner—to divine Being.

First, however, we are fated to miss our way by developing a consciousness that makes us feel free and independent, but actually betrays the eternal law of change and severs our contact with Being.

The Way of initiation means changing utterly, undergoing a mighty "conversion," and committing ourselves irrevocably to service of the Absolute. It means sacrificing everything that prevents us from serving the Absolute and unconditionally accepting everything that helps us to do so. It is a life-and-death matter. It means obeying the master, who embodies Life and so has sole and absolute authority over his students. Submission to his authority is an expression of the freedom that comes of being totally, limitlessly connected with Being—a freedom that increases day by day as the bond becomes closer.

There are three stages in human development, and the Way of initiation begins with the transition to the third. At the first stage, the self, preservation of the self, and the safe enjoyment of life's basic pleasures are the only things that matter. At the second, "others" take over—things, work, people, communities. Typical of this stage are those who have shed their selfishness and devote themselves wholly to a cause. Virtue here means having the strength to overcome inner and outer resistance bravely, selflessly, and lovingly in the "service" of the community. Dedication to this service is rooted in honor, and loss of honor means social death, exclusion from the community. The "wholly other," which transcends everything, appears at this stage in unconditional acceptance of the world's principles, systems, and laws.

At the third stage, the only things that count are "true nature" and the individual's transformation as he gradually achieves unity with divine Being embodied in his true nature. His first contact with it comes when the Absolute erupts commandingly into consciousness. He now senses otherworldly Life, not merely as the right to life or the duty of serving the world, but also as a promise and summons, telling him to seek union with the divine and to serve it.

The Way of initiation is the way on which we realize that we have gone astray and lost contact with our eternal origin, and on which we then try to restore that contact. It is the way on which, having never conceived of ourselves as manifesting Being, we first and increasingly discover that we have potential power to do just that—and acquire the strength to use it. This Way demands a total change of direction. It demands death and rebirth.

There are two developmental stages on the Way of initiation. At the first, a repeated letting go of the old and letting in of the new gradually brings us into a state where we become permeable to our own true nature and its inbuilt law of change. Nothing can be pure enough to manifest Being unless it is permeable in this sense. This stage is the way to the Way. At the second stage, we become a perfect medium, achieve permeable form and formed permeability—and ourselves become the Way.

As initiation, the Way is the process in which Life, having once been missed, now takes on form in a preordained sequence of steps and stages, and finally breaks through. Before this can happen, a special experience must have shown us our true nature and destiny, and we must ourselves be willing to sacrifice everything to fulfill the destiny it has revealed.

The Way is a step-by-step, stage-by-stage transformation, and its purpose is the clear revelation of Being in human form. The transformation itself is effected in a prolonged process of conscious contact and union with the potential, and this means that the actual must repeatedly be sacrificed. "Union" never means simply the possibility of the Absolute manifesting itself in a spiritual and intellectual sense—it also means the obligation of bearing physical witness to it in a here-and-now form.

On the Way, the eternal alternation of Yin and Yang becomes conscious and is willed, as we learn to leave all the old forms behind and to let new ones in. The Way is long and hard until the shifting balance of Yin and Yang generates the polar rhythm in which Tao can live itself out unchecked.

The steps we take on the Way of initiation are not something that people have dreamed up and thought out rationally. They implement a certain law of change that is written into us and that we can and must fulfill at a certain stage in our development. The Way is Life, living out its truth in human shape. The words "I am the Way, the Truth and the Life" may have had a special meaning when Christ used them of himself, but they are also written into every living creature. Our true nature is not an indwelling image but our own indwelling Way. It is an innate sequence that we are fated to follow in maturing to a state in which nothing is left to check the ongoing process of change that progressively perfects us as mediums. At this point we are truly on the *Way* for the first time—indeed, we have become the Way ourselves.

The way to the Way begins at a threshold that can only be crossed by leaping to another level. We reach that threshold when carrying on in the same old direction or continuing to live in the same old way would mean the end—stasis, paralysis, or all-consuming apathy and sloth. We reach it when the nearness of death makes true nature rebel—when we have come to a dead end and must take the leap that carries us past it.

Entering on the Way depends on the Absolute's bursting into our ordinary life—and it also depends on recognizing that experience for what it is, sensing the promise it contains, and accepting the obligations it imposes.

Many things can set us on the way to the Way. Whenever we choose a way for ourselves, set off in pursuit of a goal and fail to achieve it, that failure pulls us up, makes us think again and ask ourselves: "Could I be on quite the wrong track?" In every worldly failure the inner master is telling us to remember the only thing that matters—is telling us to aim at contact with the Absolute.

The *Way* is Life's way of achieving conscious form in human beings and exists only when reason's stifling hold has been broken. There are three stages in this process. At the first, or pre-rational, stage, Life unconsciously takes on appropriate form. Without doing anything and without knowing what is happening, we grow "biologically" out of Life's strength, order, and unity. At the second, or rational, stage, we systematically seek to impose on Life a meaning and a form of our own making—mastering nature, shaping the world, creating, ordering, sharing intellectual values, and living in harmonious community with others. The third stage comes only when our vision of reality transcends objective consciousness and we become able to devote, not only our self-willed individuality, but also our selfless, idealistic worldly instincts, to the service of Being, which is coming to awareness in us and perpetually remaking us. At this point Being itself becomes the center and source of meaning and we are on the way to our true self. From now on, anything we do to serve the world is also an opportunity to help the One reveal itself.

As long as we have not ourselves been seized by Being, we seek fulfillment in valid worldly form, creating a series of more or less perfect structures that seem to give logical, aesthetic, and ethical principles a durable form. At this stage, we find happiness, meaning, and security in these structures, in the midst of the sufferings and vicissitudes of our everyday existence. But our very talent for "objectivity" and our belief that we can always turn transience into permanence are the source of a danger—the danger of standing still ourselves. The more successfully we use these seemingly durable values to mask our unconscious anguish at failing to realize our true self, and the more we cling to them, the harder it becomes to find our way back to our real way—the Way of transformation and maturity.

Objective human consciousness reduces absolute infinity to an endless finite series, and timeless Being to something that lasts forever. The spirit that does this is working against Life, and it turns a person into an enemy of Life when it penetrates that person's inner self. Instead of moving on, he or she freezes on the spot. But this itself can save him or her if the pain inflicted on true nature by stasis again brings the truth of Life to light. At this point the congealing world of objects becomes a painful ground and source for realization of what the subject is really meant to do. What seemed a graveyard becomes a garden as Life flowers anew and comes to consciousness.

The Way of initiation starts with a wholly new vision of life—a Copernican revelation—when Being experienced shows us that we and our world are not the center of the universe but are rotating around another center and must now do so consciously. But this realization does not mark the start of the Way unless it comes as a shattering experience, is instantly sensed as practical obligation and evident meaning, and is accepted in a spirit of selfless commitment as the vital center of existence. To enter on the Way, it is not enough to start believing that Being is the true center; we must experience it, accept it, and will it as the true center deep within ourselves. Only if we do that will we also come to see the persistent, self-assertive, pain-fleeing ego, with its shallow worldly pleasures and its self-protective systems, for what it really is: something that hurts us and that threatens and betrays the only thing that matters.

The Way has no goal, no destination to be reached. It is itself the goal. As beginners we may imagine that someday, somewhere, we will arrive, but it is our imagined goal's constant recession that eventually shows us that we are making progress—*if* we are making progress—and suddenly makes us realize that, if we continue to advance, we have already reached the goal in the absolute movement of ongoing change. When we become a part of perpetual flux, a great peace enters and possesses us. The concept of a goal to be reached belongs to the world of the objectively defining ego, and breaking—that is, relinquishing—the power of that ego is our first task upon the Way.

There are two kinds of stillness: the stillness of death, in which all movement ceases, and the stillness of life, in which nothing is left to check the movement of change.

The Way allows us to achieve union with divine Life and to preserve it in the here-and-now world. It consists of three parallel tracks: ongoing *development of the faculty* that increasingly enables us to experience the Absolute present in ourselves and in everything else and to grasp its true significance; *insight into the conditions* that help us to achieve union with the Absolute or prevent us from doing so; and practice, that is, *exercises aimed at dismantling* everything that obstructs this union and fostering everything that makes it possible.*
Unconsciously, the desire to be acknowledged and assisted in these three areas is always a part of the call for the master.

The aim of every practice focused on the Way is to make adepts perfect mediums—to enable them to perceive Being, present in their own true nature, and allow it to manifest itself in them and through them in the world.

The real center, on which everything turns, to which everything must be related, and in which everything originates, has been described in various ways, but it cannot truly be named. It is always experienced, however, as a "you"—as personified challenge, salvation, yardstick, compass, and shaping principle. Whether we call it God, Life, divine Being, Buddha, Christ, or Holy Spirit; whether names like these give it a definite place in a definite theology; whether or not it has

*Cf. Karlfried Graf Dürckheim, *Überweltliches Leben in der Welt,* 2d ed. (Munich: O. W. Barth-Verlag, 1972).

taken on human contours in traditional stories and images—as the center of the Way it lies beyond words, stories, and images, and works through direct, wordless, pictureless experience as the ultimate source of strength, meaning, and security.

It is not only the full, dramatic experience of Being that has a special quality. Even the lightest contact has this quality too: a penetrating sense of the numinous, coupled with the sense of a new driving force that picks us up, absorbs us, transports and exalts us out of ourselves, and at the same time gives us back to ourselves in a very special way. Like everything we register as "holy" or "sacred," this sense of the numinous always points to dawning awareness of the Absolute's presence. It has nothing to do with conventional extremes of happiness or fear. In it, we are touched by the supra-worldly—the ungraspable something that is basically with us all the time, driving us on and holding us back, calling us out of and throwing us back upon ourselves, questioning and affirming us, destroying us and giving birth to us anew. This is why the numinous is at once fascinating and terrible, and both to the same end—shaping us so that Life can reveal itself, ever more purely and ever more directly, in us and through us in the world. The eternal master is at work in this kind of numinous contact, calling us to the Way and keeping us on it. We long for his call from the depths of our true nature. Our call is, however, the master's call, which is registered first in our longing and then in our will. His call is the call of our own true nature.

The numinous is, in fact, the basic quality of all religious experience. A significant difference, however, is whether it merely confirms, informs, and fertilizes a belief—or shows that a person is in tune with true nature and the Way, and spurs him on in his personal efforts to change in a manner consonant with Being.

The bundled energy of life, repressed and clamoring for expression, obscures the Way to perfect mediumship. This energy is negative, and we call it the "shadow." It expresses itself in wrong impulses and forces its way destructively to the surface. There are two methods we can use to master these evil forces and make them contribute to our transformation on the Way. One is the psychological method: this involves identifying the roots of repression and allowing its energy to express itself in liberating, helpful ways. The other is "asceticism"; this means relating to God in a total sense and sacrificing our own harmful urges and demands with true humility. This sacrifice is genuine only when the ego itself is unconditionally sacrificed. This is the kind of action that effects total change—an action that is freely performed for God's sake and that wins new life by accepting death. There can be no progress on the Way without self-discipline. When we identify the shadow, and find that we can turn it into something positive, this discovery does not mean that the old practices—fasting, prayer, abstinence, and mortification of the flesh—are worthless. The gods have made effort the price of virtue, and self-sacrifice and death the price of transformation. The Absolute never purifies and liberates us in the deepest sense unless we help it to do so.

The Way of initiation is not a straight line but a spiral—a spiral of centripetal and centrifugal forces. It involves movement from the periphery to the center, and from the center to the periphery. It leads from the periphery to the center, from infinite distance to the innermost heart, and then back to the periphery.

We have a constant sense of being drawn, driven, and summoned to the center, and then released back into the world outside. The Whole, which we ourselves are, breathes in this movement and reflects itself in our uniqueness. It is only in this out-in rhythm—this pendulum movement that carries us out of ourselves and then back to our own center—that we become what we really are.

We experience our own center in its vital connection with everything around us—as the wellspring and home of all the things that have meaning for us and meaning in our world. These things are, in fact, the finite reflections of our true nature, striving to manifest itself in space and time. In this sense, the periphery serves as a theater where the true center can emerge and take on form, but the periphery also threatens to destroy the center—just as the center poses a redeeming threat to the periphery. The center can dissipate in the periphery, and the periphery faces the "shock" of coming to a seeming dead end in the center. Each lives from the threat that it faces in the other. Both owe their vital energy to the fact that no pause, no standing still, is permitted in the to-and-fro movement between them.

Growing into one's ultimate center is never a steady process, and the Way is not an even one. It begins with a shock, and there are countless snares, obstacles, and pitfalls that must be overcome along it. Again and again, students relapse from the new dimension into their natural ego's ways and habits—and a total change, a perilous leap, is always needed to carry them up to the center again. The qualities they need here are totally different from those required by the everyday world, and this is why the world itself changes utterly when Being dawns in them. Because they themselves are different, they see, seek, and love differently—and see, seek, and love *different things.*

The leap into the other dimension involves letting go, giving up, and often destroying the things that bind us to the world, and doing this lets us live from a new strength, in a new meaning-system, and in a new love. Worldly love ties us down, fuses us with the love object, and makes us incapable of letting it go. Absolute love is the unity and union experienced in true nature, and freedom experienced within the contingent—an experience in which nothing is clung to.

Superficially, someone who is on the way to the Way may retain his old ties. Basically, however, he is free of them. They no longer serve as yardstick or signpost, and he gives them up instantly when they come between him and the Way.

Ultimately, the Way that concerns us here is not a way we travel but a way that travels us. We do not enter the Way—one day, the Way enters us and takes over. Action and effort are needed on the way to the Way. Once we reach it, however, it seizes us and asks nothing of us but compliance, a willingness to be traveled by it.

The only effort needed on the Way is that of resisting any temptation to try to determine the direction ourselves—even with paradise as our destination. If we see the Way in our own terms and make a conscious attempt to maintain the right heading, then we have already lost it. All we have to do as we approach it is to stay vigilant, listen, obey, and hold the ego—even the well-meaning, "salvation-seeking" ego—firmly in check whenever it tries to interfere.

The Way that travels us is the everlasting master as way. He is the real Self within us, the Whole that was there from the start (although we must also make it real), has now come to life within us, rebels whenever we lose sight of or betray it, and remakes itself afresh in a constantly renewed, forward-pointing process. This is the master for whom we are calling and who is constantly calling us. When we call the master, we are really echoing the eternal master's everlasting summons to us—indeed, it is only when we have heard him that we call him.

Of course, once the Way has seized us we must keep moving, cling to nothing, and let nothing hold us back. We are constantly tempted, however, to stay where the staying is "good." To this extent, we are never released from the responsibility of keeping on the move and are always expected to fulfill the Way consciously. The freedom we have is the freedom to say yes or no to the options in front of us: to the movement of Life that pushes us on to further change or to the movement of the ego that seeks security and stasis.

If we are serious about the Way, we must learn to leave everything behind—and not once, but again and again. This brings us into the void. But the void is empty in the right way only when it signifies the door to fullness, and when giving up the old form lets in the new one.

The actual must yield and make way for the possible. Multiplicity must fall silent before fullness can be heard. It is up to us to ensure that the void, from which the new can emerge, does not become a bottomless, all-devouring pit, but remains the mother-ground and matrix in which the new can take root and flower.

A little bird perches on a leafless branch stretching into emptiness (a motif treated by great painters of all countries and periods). In this way, the bird gives emptiness a voice—and emptiness does likewise for the bird.

The infinite is woken in the individual by the finite, which contradicts it, and the finite finds its true nature in the infinite, which also contradicts it.

Life generates a comprehensive range of forms, each distinct and complete in itself (Yang), and absorbs them back into the great All-One (Yin). Life's adversary destroys it by arresting its movement at either end of the process—paralyzing it at the point where form is consummated, or dissipating it at the point where form merges with the All-One. The master speaks with the voice of the living whole that lives itself out in polar oscillation and never stands still. He calls completed form back into its primal matrix and summons this matrix to rebirth in form. In the living process, both movements are fused in one.

A great moment comes in our life when we are suddenly given the grace to see that everything that happens in and around us is a part of Being's omnipotent effort to manifest itself in space and time. This insight may also be accompanied by horrified realization of the extent to which we are actually preventing it from doing so in our own human world. This experience may spark the great conversion, in which we become servants of Being.

In human consciousness, Life comes to awareness of itself in the perils that beset its coming to form. In failing to bring Life to form, we become aware of the wholeness that Life intends us to have: we become aware of its depth when we threaten to stagnate, of its limitations only when we go beyond them, and of its possibilities only when we essay the

84

impossible. Whenever the eternal master seizes us as Way, he harries us from our fixed positions to a point of transition—and beyond. The leap of transition signifies both destruction and new life.

Progressing on the way to the Way involves constantly losing and recovering wholeness by perceiving and accepting the antitheses contained in it: heaven and earth, form and formlessness, consciousness and unconsciousness, male and female. In the human consciousness these opposites are perpetually separating out, confronting and warring on each other, before joining again to form new wholes. The more deeply a person senses the dangers inherent in this process, looks them in the face, and temporarily accepts them, the more vital and truer to true nature will be the whole that grows out of their reconciliation, and the more faithfully the process of becoming will reflect Life as the ever-creating, ever-redeeming spirit. The eternal master is never content to let us pause, to enjoy smooth harmony and peace. The moment we show signs of settling down, he chases us back onto the Way.

Christ the Master

For the Christian West, the eternal master is historically personified in Jesus Christ, in whom the idea of the master is uniquely realized and in whom all the attributes of true masters everywhere are present and combined.

For the believing Christian, Jesus Christ, the Son of God, who died and rose again for us, is uniquely holy and divine—but the essential difference between Christ and believer is not that the believer is merely human and that Christ is both human and divine. Everything the master represents and is points to the fact that we all are—and are destined to become—both human and divine; that our superhuman true nature is our real source and core, but that our worldly existence must be suffered, lived, and fulfilled as the manifestation of it. The master's eternal task is to wake us to this core and, from it, to give us the strength that enables us to master the world and makes us independent of it.

Listening to the Gospel exposes us to the breath of the divine, wakes the eternal, and makes it resonate within us. It makes us students of the eternal master, whom we can hear within ourselves in the voice of the Holy Spirit. We live in an age of dawning awareness of the Holy Spirit's presence within us. But just as only a limited number of people have reached the stage where they can hear the inner master ("have ears to hear"), so the real meaning of the Scriptures cannot ultimately be grasped with the help of learned explanations but only through post-mental, subjective consciousness. (Christ's words were addressed to an age and a people who had not, like ourselves, passed through the rational stage.)

Living belief is a spiritual state in which the mystery speaks vitally to us because it has not been "aired," that is, exposed to the devitalizing light of reason. And so people who have made progress on the Way of initiation—who have, in other words, achieved a "consciousness" beyond reason and are increasingly open to the mystery—are on the way to the truth of Christ. They have opened themselves to their own true nature and, in so doing, have turned themselves into sounding boards for the eternal master's voice. In their call for the master they have themselves become the living answer to the Word that addresses us from everything that is.

The time has now come to rediscover the treasures of initiatory knowledge that are buried in the Christian tradition of the West—in the religious experience and wisdom of the primitive Christians, the early Christian anchorites and monks, the medieval mystics, and the alchemists and "initiates," with their countless circles and secret orders. Here we shall have to make a distinction between mystical experience and the Way of initiation, which includes mystical experience but systematically processes and builds on it. The call for the master is not simply the call for mystical experience but is also the call for guidance on a way of change that allows us to break through to the Absolute and—if we do so—to become mediums with power to give the Absolute form in the world. This process makes us in the fullest sense vessels for divine Being—open to receive it, shaped to retain it, and able to pour it out again. We must know that we, like the everyday life that surrounds us, are ourselves the divine Word in hidden form, and be able to witness to that fact. The eternal master within us and the here-and-now master outside both teach us to identify the concealing element and turn it into a transparent medium for the infinite in the finite. This Way will bring us an increasing sense of Christ's presence as our eternal master, and the command to see the world and love others "in Christ" will fulfill itself almost as a matter of course in our lives once we have matured to the truth of what we really are and live from it.

The Voice
of the Master
in Everyday Life

When we have entered on the way to the Way and are determined to serve Life in the everyday, then the everyday can itself become our master on the inner way. Once we know how to listen for it, we hear the inner master's voice everywhere: for example, in the way we use our body, perform daily actions, confront the ups and downs of life, react to our own highs and lows, and resist or give in to the lures and temptations of the world. Loudly or softly, it speaks out unmistakably and tells us whether we are advancing on the Way or standing still, or whether, at that very moment, we are on the point of going astray and betraying ourselves. Once we have woken to the Way we are always aware that our real task is preparing to become perfect mediums, and the voice of conscience, in which the master speaks to us, is never silent. For the true student, everything that happens in daily life is a test.

When we are coping with "outside" life and destiny we are constantly tempted to forget the real meaning of our existence. The world offers us countless opportunities, temptations, and dangers of narrowing our focus down from the Absolute to the ego's close-up objectives, either bad or even well-meaning and "good." Instead of heeding our true nature's anguish at estrangement from Being, we keep coming back to the anguish caused us by our worldly "situation." Coming to terms with this "natural" anguish is also, however, a central factor on the Way. When we serve Life, we are not allowed to take the experience that gives us liberating contact with the higher world as a pretext for spurning this one and pitching our tents on the opposite shore; for our life's business is to make room for the otherworldly in the world. We need worldly power to do this, and we can gain that power only by repeatedly putting the inner form won through contact with Being—that is, by internally coming to terms with our true nature—at risk in externally coming to terms with the world. And we must also follow our shadows. If we do this, our inner and outer courage or cowardice will soon tell us whether we are really following the Way and the master's uncompromising guidance. When we are really on the way to the Way, any pause, any straying from the path, immediately wakes the master's warning voice. But we also hear his approval when we "are there" in the right way, and hear him encouraging us and urging us on whenever a new approach to the Way presents itself and we have doubts about taking it or are afraid to do so. And when our way of "being there" is really the right one, we sense it deep inside in a vital, bright, approving stillness—a stillness beyond "psychic movement" and beyond the world's calm or commotion. Something similar happens in profound meditation when an outside noise that at first disturbs us mysteriously becomes the background to an inner tranquillity—a tranquillity that has nothing to do with noise or silence, but lies beyond both.

Really to wake to the Way is to reach a rare and lofty stage of human development. People today, for whom "right living" is summed up in three things—success, productivity, and good behavior—are light-years away from it. But the clearer-sighted among them are no longer really happy with all this, and indeed feel the painful pressure of all the genuinely important things that the world forces them to forget. This is why it is vital to try to wake the conscience from which wholeness and true nature speak. An intellectual grasp of the sublime insights and maxims that guide us toward full selfhood, toward becoming all-round human beings, is not enough. They must be physically real, and we must be able to tell whether we are succeeding or failing on the path to mediumship from our bodily condition, posture, breathing, tension and relaxation, and even the most trivial everyday events and the specific job we do. It is precisely into those areas that the "spiritual" person finds most alien and least interesting— the body, the most ordinary everyday actions,* and even the "lower levels" of sport and physical exercise—that the initiatory effort must reach.

Once we have woken to the Way we feel the inner master's eye fixed on us all the time. The all-seeing eye of God is no longer believed in, but is experienced personally, and everything becomes, as an Eastern saying has it, "the best of opportunities" for further progress on the inner Way. And yet, differences in character, maturity, and background mean that we all individually have areas in which we are particularly likely to catch the master's voice, or particularly inclined not to hear it. But there are three areas in which everyone who wakes to the Way hears the master's voice: in encountering his or her own *body,* in searching for the *center,* and in facing up to *death.*

*Cf. Karlfried Graf Dürckheim, *The Way of Transformation: Daily Life as a Spiritual Exercise,* trans. Ruth Lewinnek and P. L. Travers (London: Unwin Paperbacks, 1980).

The Master's Voice
in the Encounter with
the Body

The Body We Are

Nowadays, people are starting to see the human body in a radically new light. Increasingly, it is being seen as the medium in which the individual experiences and realizes himself as a person—and thus as a central factor on the Way of initiation. It is also acquiring a new significance for psychotherapists, as psychotherapy develops away from its previous pragmatic character and into an initiatory art of healing. But the process is still embryonic, and the chief problem is still that of overcoming the mind/body dualism that determines the way people are normally regarded and treated. There is nothing new in the notion that physical sickness can have psychological causes, and doctors take account of this. On the other hand, although psychotherapists without medical qualifications often consult doctors and allow for "medical factors" in their treatment, very little has really been done to bring the body into psychotherapy.

In most cases where patients are analyzed and breathing, relaxation, or movement therapy is recommended, the true personal significance of their breathing problems or tension has not been properly grasped. These various therapies are used solely as a secondary means of removing physical blocks that prevent the therapist from working on the psyche! The attitude is: "While they're tensed up like this, we can't help them." Treating physical malfunction seems to take second place to tracking down and treating the "real problem," which is thought to be solely in the "mind." All of this changes, however, when therapists stop trying simply to correct local malfunctions, remove specific complexes, and restore functional capacities by eliminating neuroses, and start looking instead at the whole person and trying to liberate and fulfill the real self. The more clearly we see that a person must also be physically "right" before this self can be fulfilled, the more dubious the body/soul dichotomy becomes, and the less likely it seems that anyone can be seen and "therapized" in isolation from the body. But what does *body* mean here? Is it "the body" of traditional medicine? By no means!

Medicine, too, is changing. Doctors are increasingly realizing today that the view that sees physical disease in isolation from the soul is a blinkered one. But what is this "soul," which they would really like to start treating too? Is it the psyche of conventional psychology? Certainly not! Depth psychology and the therapy based on it are the first significant aids to medicine here. On the other hand, medical discoveries and growing medical experience are also extending the psychotherapist's view beyond the merely psychic. (This includes some of the insights contained in the unorthodox research and treatment methods that are bundled together under the name "experience therapy.") Something that has so far seemed little more than a respectful convergence of medicine and psychology in such areas as psychosomatic medicine, where each side learns from the other, is gradually leading to the recognition of a third element, beyond the body/soul dichotomy. A new cognitional factor enters the game, for example, when even a doctor starts paying attention to "shallow breathing"—which is still by no means an illness—and seeing it, not as a symptom of chronic catarrh or a mere psychic problem, but as the expression of a *subjective* anxiety that also sets up physical tension and nervousness and stands in the way of a cure. A new insight also dawns when a psychotherapist sees that hunched shoulders are the "physical" correlative of an inner defensiveness that, because it is physical, prevents a step forward—long overdue in psychic terms—from being taken on the path to maturity.

Insights of this kind derive from observable facts, and they are generating a conception of the "person in the body" that differs significantly from the old view of human beings as variously defined combinations of body and soul, consciousness and matter. Already the question is not merely "How do body and soul fit together?" but also "How did we ever imagine they were separate?" But what secret power, what mysterious "third man," is bringing medicine and psychology together? The human individual, increasingly aware of his own *wholeness*! This new awareness is part of a general trend, a trend that is making people increasingly resentful of the worldly pressures that are functionalizing them and so threatening their wholeness and ultimately reducing them to components—bits of the world. And this resentment stems, not merely from the personally determined world-ego, but above all from otherworldly true nature. When that is suppressed, the result is an anguish that pragmatic therapy, with its emphasis on performance, cannot cure. The only answer is initiation therapy, which aims at transformation and maturity, a therapy in which doctor and patient must both listen for the inner master's voice in the body.

There is a spiritual realm that the dazzling light of science once stopped us from seeing, and the *human being* is emerging from it today—bringing with him the suppressed side of his true nature, as he *experiences* himself and *lives himself out* as a physical person in the world, as we automatically encounter him in the personal I/You relationship. But as soon as we stop to reflect on it, this direct, unthinking experience of being-in-the-world and being-in-the-world-with-others is at once overlaid by accumulating concepts that stop us from turning the deeper wisdom of direct understanding and contact into something consciously known. This is how the intellectual conception of body and soul as separate has conditioned our whole understanding of humanity, banishing everything that transcends this antithesis from scientific consciousness.

Seen as a specific someone, the individual is beyond the conceptual body/soul or body/consciousness antithesis. But individuals are always "subjects" and always physical presences. Whatever they do or feel, *they* feel and do it "bodily," or rather, as a body. And their experience of guidance on the inner Way—of the inner master's voice—is also a bodily experience.

The body that interests psychotherapy is not the body that concerns medicine. Admittedly this is true only of the psychotherapy that wants, not merely to repair suspended function, but also to help the patient *really* to become *the* person that his otherworldly *true nature* makes him. But a *person* is *real* in the *here-and-now* only in a bodily form. He is "real" only in this form, and never without it. Only in or, rather, "as" this form, can he also become the person he is basically meant to be and should be in the world. This is why we have to make a distinction between the body we are and the body we have!

The people we actually meet are never bodies or souls. It is only the defining ego's analytical eye that sees inner and outer, soul and body, as distinct realities. Holistically seen as a "you," a person is always a *subject* in bodily form, and his or her *inner* and *outer* modes of being cannot be separated.

When we see people whole, the body is not a physical organism that can be parted from the subject, and it is not an instrument serving the world-ego more or less efficiently. Rather, it is the here-and-now medium in which people subjectively *are* and become in the fullest sense themselves. It is their way of *being there* as "true nature" in the world. It is the sum total of the gestures in which they manifest themselves, express what they are, take on form and fulfill themselves in that form or fail to do so. The body they are in this sense is the mode in which they not only experience but also "embody" themselves in a manner either consistent with or contrary to their destiny, and fulfill themselves, in constant physical change, more or less in accordance with their true nature. Keeping this body "healthy" thus depends on an initiatory healing art that has nothing to do with pragmatic therapy.

Working on the body in initiation therapy is a matter of following the *basic law* of our own being, the law everyone must obey in order to be and remain a healthy human person. It is the inner master's voice that tells us that we must obey this law, and it tells us itself that becoming a *person* is our purpose. Ultimately, to be a person in this sense is to be a subject freely and consciously capable of allowing supraworldly Being, which is present in us (in our *true nature*) and striving to manifest itself, to speak through us and take on form in our worldly existence.

The basic law of our own being is thus concerned with realizing our otherworldly true nature in the world, that is, in the *body*. This is why initiation therapy is always concerned with the bodily manifestation of true nature as well. The key to obeying this law is, however, a state of mind and being whose main feature is transparency.

Transparency means "permeability." It allows us to admit Being to consciousness in such a way that we can then witness to it physically in our everyday existence. The state that engenders this quality is not simply an inner order, an order of the heart. It is also a physical order, an order of the body. It is only in both that the "order of the person" appears. It is certain that we can fulfill our human destiny only in our way of "being there" in the world—as a body—and it is equally certain that any personal therapy must extend to bodily form. This, however, means something more than looking after one's health!

Bodily health *as a person* is not the same thing as good physical health. The medical profession can make people healthier, but this does not mean that the researchers and doctors behind its successes have really seen and treated people as persons—any more than sickness, if some shred of consciousness remains, is enough to stop any human being from realizing himself or herself as a person. Often, physical suffering and imminent death are the very things that prepare us for personhood and allow us to manifest ourselves in that dimension. Good health, on the other hand, frequently distracts us from the path that leads inward.

Our bodily form is "right" when it allows Being to

show through from our true nature, and when we ourselves are "fit" in a way that enables us to witness externally to its fullness and unity, internally present in that true nature. Seeing people whole and relating the body to true nature (and its drive to self-manifestation) takes us away from the old causal approach to inner factors and opens our eyes to the significance of bodily behavior and form as expressions of self-fulfillment from true nature. And as the meaning of *diagnosis* changes, so does the meaning of *therapy,* and with it the doctor's role. He becomes companion and guide on the Way—he becomes a guru.

When the body is seen not as something that people have but as something that they are—as the sum total of the gestures in which they live themselves out, that is, express and realize themselves in a visible, external form—then this form must also point to what they really are. The implication here is twofold—it must show what the world has made them and must also show what they are in their true nature! Form in this sense also shows how and how far their bodily being connects with their true nature. In this "personal" view of the body, character is not a particular bundle of characteristics but the relationship between two types of form—the form imprinted by the world and the form intended by true nature! Whether moving or at rest, the body and the various parts of the body thus become so many signatures pointing to a subject, who is fulfilling humanity's law to a greater or lesser extent in the specific circumstances of his or her own life. The vision of the body that shifts the focus in this way to true nature's intentions has direct initiatory significance. Its concern is with personal form as a function of *true nature.*

As soon as we start looking through the outer and visible to the inner and invisible and trying to see how form and meaning relate, most of the old body/soul dichotomy vanishes. The soul then becomes the body's *meaning,* and the body the expression of the soul.* But we must go one step

*Cf. Ludwig Klages, *Der Geist als Widersacher der Seele* (Leipzig: J. A. Barth, 1929).

further and say: What we call "soul" and "body" are simply the modes in which the whole human being lives himself out as a person by being externally what he is internally, and vice versa—that is, by experiencing himself, living himself out, and embodying himself both as "inner" and "outer." There are also two elements in the "inner" self: what he has *actually* become in response to the world around him, and what he *really,* absolutely, is and should be from his true nature. Seeing a person in his body (seeing him fully and correctly as a body) is thus seeing him in terms of the worldly body/true form relationship and registering the extent to which his physical form reflects his "true nature."

Once we start "reading" the body for signatures that can be interpreted and relating individuals to what they should be, we inevitably see them, too, as the microcosmic reflection and embodiment of laws and signs that determine the universal life of which they themselves are all separate manifestations. Being and remaining healthy then automatically become a matter of respecting universal laws. This is why therapists today are instinctively seeking out the wisdom of the past, which saw the human body and the universe as a unity.

However, Being can manifest itself in a person only in that person's predestined form, and people can validly find their way to Being only by realizing the form implicit in their own true nature.

As it shifts its sights from repairing performance to fostering emergence of the true self, that is, to fusing true nature and world-ego in the sign and service of the Absolute, therapy becomes initiation therapy, and the therapist becomes a guru. Whether they know it or not, whether they mean to or not, his "patients" stop turning to him as a doctor and start turning to him as a master. But the master's way of dealing with the body is also different from the doctor's. What he sees, touches, and treats in the body is a person on the way to becoming a window for the Absolute. As a master, he takes the seeker in hand.

Therapists treating the whole person must know how

to "read" the patient's body—or external form—and see how it relates to the "true" form that shimmers through it. Similarly, the treatment they provide must attempt to foster conditions that allow the patient to achieve harmony with his true nature in his external form (as a body) too.

If the body is true nature's personal, physical mode, then it also expresses the extent to which physical form accords (or fails to accord) with true nature at any given moment. This significantly affects the holistic therapist's way of looking at people, since his or her interest is not merely in worldly performance but in the emergence of true nature. In this kind of therapy, the "personal" vision of the body is important for the therapist and equally important for the patient—indeed, self-perception in the body is vital to the patient's progress on the inner way.

When we are really on the way to the Way, we relate all our bodily sensations to the whole that is centered in our true nature and striving to fulfill itself in our body. We experience every malfunction, not as a problem of health, efficiency, or social integration, but as a problem with that self-realization as a person that our true nature demands of us. Whenever we become conscious of malfunction, we encounter the whole, the whole that calls us to "order" and is determined by Life— in other words, the inner master's voice.

But the eye and ear needed to perceive true nature in oneself and others and to read discordancies with true nature in the body's language are the privilege of the therapist who is already on the Way. And this is also the kind of therapist who leads patients to see themselves in terms of their true nature.

Reading the Body

Without being aware of it, therapists instinctively build up a picture of their patients from the way they look and act. Consciously or unconsciously, they also note progress from changes in their way of walking, shaking hands, sitting down, sitting still, looking at or past other people, and talking. All this reveals the extent to which individual patients are candid or self-concealing, open or constricted, inhibited and ill at ease or relaxed and healthily alert, accessible or reserved—and, above all, whether they are actually giving themselves or hiding behind a façade. Therapists "register" these signs unconsciously, just as we all do unthinkingly in everyday life. Their ability to spot and understand them depends on their natural talent and experience. The body's natural language is a treasure still largely undiscovered, and discovering it—that is, systematically bringing it to consciousness and building on it—is of great potential significance for diagnosis and, later, personal therapy. Considering how important body language is in practice, amazingly little attention is paid to the study and interpretation of movement, expression, and gesture in conventional therapy and therapeutic training. As soon as a therapist becomes a guru, however, he or she also develops another vision of the body, and with it a knowledge of the symptoms and signatures that point to a person's true nature.

In a general way, we all know that character and destiny, underlying nature and life experience, are reflected in the shape of the head and the features of the face—if we could only read the signs. Surely a systematic study of those signs should be part of any therapist's training? As it is, depth psychotherapy, with its overriding interest in the unconscious and the genetic factors that condition it, has unduly diverted attention from the typological conditioning factors that can also be detected in the body. These will become increasingly important as the new awareness of the body develops and the reading of bodily signs extends to cover the relationship between world-ego and true nature (between outer form and inner form).

Just as the whole body expresses the whole person in the body's language, so every part of the body expresses the person in the language of that part. This is why it is not absurd, for example, to speak of a *science of the hand*, which goes beyond experimental observation and statistical notation of certain signs and characteristics to show what they mean and why they mean it.

So far, therapy has largely ignored the language of the hand. And yet a glance at the hand can immediately tell us certain basic things about other people: whether they are naturally loving or self-centered; whether they are naturally reserved or enterprising in their dealings with the world; and whether—and this is particularly important in personal therapy, which focuses on their true nature—they possess the primal, extrasensory sensitivity that allows them to perceive the numinous. The hand also shows whether people are primarily elemental, spiritual, or intellectual; their way of experiencing and witnessing to the Absolute will vary with these factors. It shows, too, how certain surface features relate to basic impulses. None of this gives therapists a once-and-for-all picture of their patients—but it does help them avoid certain basic errors in sizing them up and assessing their potential.

Graphology is one form of therapy that involves the body. Every therapist's training should cover the basics of graphology, not merely as a diagnostic instrument but also because of its usefulness in both initiation and pragmatic therapy.

Telling people something about their handwriting is not merely telling them more about themselves. It is also encouraging them to work on themselves—particularly when their handwriting reveals "negative" characteristics such as untruthfulness, malice, concealed aggression, a repressed urge to dominate others, unfocused intellectual energy, suppressed vitality, and selfishness.

The desire "to change" that people feel when they learn certain things about their own handwriting points to "Graphotherapy" of the kind developed by my partner and colleague Maria Hippius.* However, their actual and poten-

*Cf. Maria Hippius, "Beitrag aus der Werkstatt," in *Transzendenz als Erfahrung*, ed. M. Hippius (Weilheim: O. W. Barth-Verlag, 1966).

tial relationships with the world—for example, their capacity for success, achievement, or human contact—are not the only things that their handwriting expresses. It also says something about the way in which their world-ego and true nature relate, and thus about the stage they have reached in openness to Being and readiness for the Way. When their handwriting shows them this, their inner master is also speaking to them from it.

Graphotherapy's purpose is not to improve people's handwriting but to open their eyes to the underlying attitudes expressed in particular handwriting styles and ways of forming characters. Some of these underlying attitudes can be partly changed by repeating certain actions and characters hundreds of times. Some people may come to see, for example, that their lack of contact with the world and tendency to hold it at arm's length are reflected in handwriting that slopes to the left. They can build on this insight and start to make their characters lean to the right, not for their writing's sake, but for their own. This is very hard at first—so hard indeed, that it may seem impossible and even exasperate or frighten them. If they nonetheless persevere with the exercise—perhaps turning out thousands of loops that slope to the right—concentrate completely on what they are doing, and do it meditatively, they may then find that the self opens up in an unexpected way. People who are "on the Way" may find graphology particularly useful in opening up new fields for self-knowledge and development, for their handwriting can tell them how far the person they really are and should be has emerged or is blocked by the ego. In this case the inner master speaks to them from their own handwriting.

The language of the body in movement has both diagnostic and therapeutic possibilities. People can use it to work on their outer form entirely from the inside, gradually perfecting themselves as vessels for divine Being, which is striving to manifest itself in and through them. A living form is a form in movement, and the sum total of these movements always expresses and realizes the person incorporated in them. Any personal therapy that really sees the person in the body also sees the discrepancy between what people are externally and what they are in their true nature. Any merely worldly, habitual façade that distorts and obscures true nature (is not, in other words, the result of organic damage) must be recognized as something that prevents them from attaining their intended form, and they can and must work from the inside to remove it.

Movement therapy is the most helpful way of harnessing the knowledge and practice of expressive movement. When the therapist focuses on the emergent person, the body in movement provides important clues to diagnosis and to guidance on the Way of initiation. A physiotherapist who knows something about initiation therapy can watch the way people stand or walk and, in a matter of hours, tell them—more important, make them understand—things that straight psychoanalysis would often need months, if not years, to bring to light. Information of this kind immediately affects the patient's body because it comes *from* it! The practiced eye immediately sees where certain people are falling short of the form intended for them by their true nature, and are thus missing and living past themselves—in other words, living in contradiction to their true form. This is also, and particularly, true of the relationship between the male and female elements in ourselves, as we actually live it. But self-experience in the body can and must also develop into self-diagnosis and self-therapy.

In initiation therapy, *dance* can play a special part in helping us to achieve self-awareness and fulfill ourselves from our true nature—particularly when it comes to finding our very own, personal rhythm. A person's deepest self may well try to express itself most clearly in rhythm. Rhythm here means something very different from "tempo" or "beat." It means a characteristic and essential form that continuously recurs in similar movements and gestures, of which a certain tempo is only one feature. When we are on the Way, we hear the master's warning voice not only when our way of moving is out of step with our own rhythm, but also when our way of living is off.

No one who has seen a dancing person's realization of his inability to *give himself completely* to what he is doing, and watched as that person tries various rhythms and suddenly finds himself *in the dance,* can forget the other's obvious delight in finding *his* rhythm. Everything that goes toward determining correct overall posture—the balance between heaven and earth, male and female, Yin and Yang, the world outside and the world within—is revealed in the way people walk, and even more so in the way they dance. In dance, it is comparatively easy to make them aware, for example, of the deceptive "soaring" that deprives them of contact with the earth, or the soul-less weight that pins them to it—and this awareness carries an impetus toward self-change in movement. In personal therapy, this change centers on achieving the ability to become, feel, be, and remain their true selves—in other words, to manifest themselves ever more clearly in a movement pattern that is valid for them because it accords with their personal true nature. In this very pattern, they are also able to become increasingly aware of their share in divine Being and prove themselves in it.

"Every living creature must manifest itself, must express its form and mobility in total freedom and fullness as whatever it *is,* must rejoice in what it is in an ongoing game with itself, and in being itself taste the joy of Being in the world.

"When a person succeeds in being totally, truly himself (that is, a living archetype), then he is no longer merely himself: the barrier vanishes and he joins in the everlasting game of the living principles and powers of Being—indeed, he is swallowed by eternity, absorbed into God.

"A person can be himself only when the miracle of Being, the Divine, has seized and liberated him into an attitude in which the primal unconsciously manifests itself, because the world's All-Being is reflected in it."*

The Mask of Community

Anyone who truly belongs to a community has certain distinctive ways of speaking and moving that reflect it. These habits are generated by the group's collective ethos and express its character in all the people who belong to it, but they can also screen their own ways of expressing themselves so completely that they actively cut them off from selfhood.

There are certain ways of behaving, treating others, controlling oneself and letting oneself go, moving one's hands, looking, walking, and, above all, speaking that always go with membership in a certain group. All of this can be part of a group's collective "style." But there is a subtle distinction between style that leaves the individual element unimpeded and the communally determined "superstructure" that substitutes for individual personality or screens it out. Thus, languages and, even more, dialects express certain tribal features—and, far from stifling the personal form and individuality of the people who speak them, they articulate those values in the country's style. There are also, however, collective images and jargons that distort individuality and debase personality.

Communal behavior patterns are always expressed and rooted in a special type of self-consciousness compounded of self, shared values, and "us" (the group)—and they often appear in *exclusive* attitudes. Once the individual reaches a certain stage, they can hinder his or her development. Every age has a certain physical form and certain ways of moving. At every age, however, there are also exaggerations and accretions that specifically distort the form proper to that age. Even

*W. F. Otto, *Menschengestalt und Tanz* (Munich: Rinn, 1956), pp. 15, 18, 20.

children can display a fatal artificial childishness, for example, when they imitate the "baby talk" of adults and follow "accepted" patterns of kindergarten behavior. Later, the natural behavior patterns of puberty can tip over into open boorishness. The provocative horseplay of members of certain student fraternities provides another example. There are also the mannerisms (cultivated to start with, but often deeply ingrained) that go with certain professions (for example, teachers, priests, and soldiers)—what the French call *déformations professionnelles*. Every rank and position in the community tends to carry typical ways of behaving that hide the true self. Examples include the devoted clerk or servant, the overscrupulous government employee, the loudmouthed executive with countless underlings and one "big boss" above him, and, right at the top, the company president, who has absolute power, can give his ego free rein, and, for that very reason, often misses his true self.

The more clearly a therapist sees the *bodily* form of his patient's persona, the more sharply he senses the shadow behind every communal mask and the more acutely he perceives, behind façade and shadow, the blocked inner form that must ultimately be revealed in a specific outer form. Most behavior patterns dictated by groups are totally unconscious. But anyone who is on the way (and this always means on *his own* way too) must develop an instinct for imposed externals. The closer he is to his own true nature, the more deceptive these externals—for example, conventional elements in posture, voice, and gesture—will seem to him. The initiation therapist steadily refines his own feeling for the ways in which group influence can prevent individuals from attaining their true form, and he knows how to wake this feeling in his patients too. The more truly a seeker steps out on the way to the Way, the more instinctively he both sees that his way of living contradicts the inner truth, and hears, in the language of the body calling him to order, the inner master's voice. And so dawning awareness of the bodily form conditioned by the group paves the way for growing consciousness and realization of the outer form proper to true nature.

Stereotypes

Until they develop an instinct for the personal form they are meant to have and must realize, people are always at the mercy of stereotypes. Parental notions of upbringing, young people's magazines, films, sport, fashion, and the spirit of the age all help to create these stereotypes. Nowadays, the old ideals— "brightness" in boys, "gentleness" in girls—have stopped shaping the perceptions and attitudes of the young. New, up-to-date models—hippies, punks, rockers, dropouts—take their place at a very early age. But the stereotypes of the lady, the gentleman (or whatever counts as such), the outdoor type, the rebel, the sports star, and other ideals still persist beside them. These stereotypes often mark stages on the Way, but the exaggerations, regressions, and distortions to which they frequently give rise can falsify our natural way of expressing ourselves and prevent us from developing attitudes that accord with our true nature. Once we wake to that true nature we develop a new instinct for the ways in which we can miss it, and these stereotypes lose their hold. The commonest ideal today is personified in people who are open, honest, free, and uninhibited, stand bravely up for themselves and their beliefs, and are simply, naturally themselves—who are truly human human beings. Of all stereotypes, this is the most helpful in attaining selfhood from true nature!

Inherited patterning, organic damage that imitation of others helps to master, and painful experiences that leave defensive reactions as their legacy—all of these can make us likelier to slip, without realizing it, into a ready-made mold that takes over, makes us forget our real self and the stage we should be reaching, and forces us into a role that is totally at odds with what we really are. There is also a tendency for people with certain "temperaments" to seek out roles that give those temperaments full play—and thus encourage one-sidedness. This is why people with "lively" temperaments often turn into "adventurers," while others with "heavier" temperaments become "solid citizens"* ("lively" and "heavy" in this sense already denote specific aspects of a person's human form). Similarly, the introvert may in certain circumstances play the part of a hermit, the extrovert that of a man of the world, and so on.

People who realize that their individuality is being stifled by a stereotype never feel impelled to throw it off unless the bodily conscience that is grounded in their true nature has woken and the bodily form that matches that true nature enters their inner consciousness. Stereotypes of this kind often fill the vacuum when the individual ego is actually missing and prevent true nature from showing through. Conversely, awareness of these stereotypes often helps people to see the direction in which their true nature is guiding them.

The *physical manifestations of archetypal principles* must not be confused with collective behavior patterns or with stereotypes. What sets them apart is the fact that their supra-personal imagistic force has its roots in the Absolute. They are the positive or negative aspects of a male or female (the Great Mother) power that can take us over completely. Whenever an archetypal principle seizes us in this way, all our strengths and talents—as well as the supra-personal energies in which we share—are secretly "configured" and work together toward a certain form. To become fully conscious, this form must then be experienced in bodily shape. This can make us aware of our own inner form's supra-personal significance and open our eyes to the perilous spell that lies over us. It can also make us aware that inner form obliges us both to act in certain ways and, because it accords with our true nature, to realize it in a corresponding outer form.

But transformation in the body means more than this. There is a tradition—old, but still useful and widely accepted—that sees human beings in terms of three levels: nature, spirit, and intellect. Whatever we make of these weighty concepts, they undoubtedly point to three dimensions that are

*See W. Welzig, *Beispielhafte Figuren* (Graz/Cologne: Böhlau, 1963).

both typologically and genetically significant. There are definitely people who are close to nature and at one with it, while others exist more in spiritual experience or the intellect. In each case this is expressed in the whole body, as it is in the face, the parts of the body (hands), and the way a person writes. At the same time, these three levels are all present in every human being, and this means that they also reflect a developmental process that we are expected, in a general sense, to follow. We all have a personal formula that allows us to bring them into harmony—into *our* harmony. The inner master guides us toward this formula, showing us if and how we can transcend our original links with the natural and elemental, develop a new inwardness, breathe spirit into the world, and ultimately grow beyond and out of the spiritual into the realm of absolute mind, where nature and the inner workings of our own spirit are forgotten and all that matters is experience and manifestation of the Absolute in an outer form matching our true nature.

Just as the body "types" a person, it also shows whether he or she belongs on the natural, spiritual, or intellectual level. Therapists must "see" who they are dealing with. Each of the levels has its own health, its own potential beauty, and its own potential way of mediating the Absolute. With every step taken on the path to "infusion with the spirit," the body changes materiality, refining away from its initial coarseness and ultimately becoming a kind of ethereal pointer to another dimension that appears in, shines through, or radiates from it. Therapists must be alive to the various forms and levels of nature, spirit, and intellect that can seek and find expression in the human body, and must focus on them in dealing with their patients. To do this, they must first be aware of their own nature and level. This is essential if they are to see and treat them—even if the treatment is wordless—in a manner appropriate to the level that they "see" in them, and not assign their patients to the wrong form or drive them onto a level beyond their reach or keep them on a level they should leave behind.

By *wordless treatment* we mean that the therapist wakes

the inner master and allows him to start working in the patients. This is not just something that therapists should do, but something we all should do whenever we find ourselves in full, responsible contact with another human being. We can only do it, however, if we are ourselves students of the everlasting master and if the inner master is at work in us. Then we, too, can function as masters.

Practice

Bringing the body into therapy and guidance on the Way also means practice, which denotes any exercise that sets out to turn the body into a window for the Absolute.

Personal mediumship means being present from Being and for it. We are persons in the full sense only when Being sounds through us without our realizing it and when our own way of "being there" reflects an inwardness consciously rooted in true nature. This inwardness always includes our awareness of ourselves as a body more or less transparent for Being, that is, for our own true nature. We can be consciously present from our true nature only in a body that allows that true nature to show through.

True nature is the mode in which Life is present in the individual, and is thus life itself. *Life* in this sense always means movement and change in the everlasting rhythm of coming into being and ceasing to be. This is why true nature is present in us, not simply as an innate form, but also as an innate process or Way. True nature is a person's own *law of becoming,* and can fulfill itself only in a form of which change is the essence. The predisposition to mediumship is at work in this law as necessity, promise, and obligation, but fulfillment is obstructed, and the process of change that points to "being on the Way" is arrested, when the *world-ego* cuts loose from Being, takes over, and shuts true nature out; for this is an ego that, in knowledge and action, is always circling a fixed point.

Its will to permanence makes it cling to fixed systems and block every change. Life, on the other hand, is constantly creating and constantly redeeming, and it manifests itself in flux and change. In a healthy person it shows in an endless succession of formal variations. Indeed, a person is physically "transparent" when his or her outer form guarantees this process of change. And so the aim of every exercise that qualifies as practice is to achieve a bodily state that allows the process to take place and ensures that it does so.

Personal form in this sense is determined by *overall posture, breathing,* and the *inner balance of tensions* (the inner relationship between tension and relaxation). What initiation therapy sees in all of this is not bodily function but psychophysically neutral manifestations of the person. The rightness or wrongness of posture, breathing, and tension depends on the extent to which they match our own basic law and help or hinder us on the path to mediumship. The world-ego's dominance is the main cause of their being wrong. That ego's self-assertion is admittedly a part of being human, but as soon as it tries to take over it prevents us from maturing out of our true nature. Its dominance is reflected in incorrect posture, shallow breathing, and an alternate tightening up and letting go that replaces the right balance of tension and relaxation.

Practicing toward the right state of mind and body primarily means trying to anchor oneself in the right *center,* to achieve the right center of gravity. This is located in the pelvis/stomach region. In "personal" terms, these are not simply parts of the body but denote the maternal region of change, the "spiritual soil" that absorbs fixed forms and melts them down or makes them over, releasing them into new forms and linking us with the forces of the cosmos as it does so. To reach this center is thus to escape the ego's tightening carapace and to be liberated into a new form that grows out of true nature. This is why the "vital center," which the Japanese term *Hara,* is universally important.*

*Cf. Dürckheim, *Hara: The Vital Center of Man.* trans. Sylvia-Monica von Kospoth and Estelle Healey (London: Unwin Paperbacks, 1977).

There are countless situations in which we can go wrong: we can go wrong at the elementary stage, as a natural *ego* focused on bare survival; we can go wrong as a worldly *personality* focused on permanence, service, and love as the world understands them; and we can go wrong as a *person* for whom transformation and the mediation of the Absolute are the things that count. One of the commonest reasons for failing the test, when it comes, is falling out of our own center, losing contact with true nature, on which the world has no hold, taking fright, and imagining that we must do everything ourselves. The all-determining, self-assertive ego casts its spell, and the things we have, know, and can do are no longer there when we need them, for we are ourselves obstructing the forces of the deep. Astonishing though it seems at first, this explains why finding and fixing the right center of gravity *(Hara)* is a universal remedy, as useful in the everyday world as it is on the Way to maturing from true nature.

Three things can stop us from achieving the "right" form (a form that accords with our true nature) and finding salvation: *going rigid, letting go,* and *giving up.* Winning through to health, overcoming worldly weakness, and progressing on the path to mediumship are prevented or made harder by these attitudes, all of which show that contact with our true nature has been lost. This loss is reflected in a lack of confidence, the absence of a sense of duty toward form, and in ego-hardened persistence in saying no to Life. Each of these kinds of resistance indicates that we are lost in the world-ego and out of touch with our true nature. All three aberrations are reflected in certain ingrained gestures. And so working on the right center means practicing gestures that both express and generate confidence in the Absolute, a sense of the need to achieve the form dictated by our true nature, and a renewed affirmation of Life. This is also the meaning of all personal body therapy and of all the exercises we do to become mediums for Being. It is in sensing and failing to sense this mediumship in our own body that we meet the inner master.

The Inner Master
in the Center's Voice

"La Bonne Assiette"

Significantly, the French say "Il n'est pas dans son assiette"
("He's not in his seat") of anyone who is not quite himself,
not quite together, not quite in balance. More specifically, this
means that he is irritable, touchy, reacts sharply to criticism,
finds it hard to concentrate, and is unsettled, easily upset, and
unrelaxed—is, in short, out of sorts or, one could also say, off
center! This already gives a fair idea of what being "centered"
or "not centered" means. But what has this got to do with
sitting? What exactly is this *assiette*? *Assiette* also means "plate"
or "pelvis." And so it could also be said that someone who is
off form and not his normal self is not "in his pelvis"!

Horseriders also use the term *seat*. A good rider is said
to have a "good seat." He sits correctly in his center, in his
pelvis, and this gives him a genuine feeling for his horse and
allows him to control it gently, but completely. The horse
responds obediently to the slightest pressure, while the centered rider can follow its movements easily, is firmly anchored
in the saddle, and cannot be knocked off balance or thrown.
Both horse and rider are focused on the rider's center, in
which he sits firmly—sitting, in a general sense, correctly in
himself. The right center exemplified here denotes an attitude
in which the whole person is at one with himself and the
world, controls the situation in a very special way, and is
totally, freely present as "himself." The example of the rider
shows that "being in one's center" is a personal matter and has
nothing to do with the body/soul antithesis—it is a person's
mode of *being* in the world. The more we explore this special
mode of being, the clearer it becomes that we are really centered only when we live from something that transcends the

everyday but in which we share in our true nature. This deepest, most personal of centers speaks to us in the inner master's voice, and we try to reach it on our way to the Way. If we are genuinely launched on that way, gentle signs of encouragement or warning from the inner master tell us whether or not we are on the right track.

The World—Personal and Objective Views

There are two ways of looking at the world: objectively and personally. The view we take determines the significance of everything else—and also of the center.

When we take the objective view, we try to see the world "as it is" and to ignore the ways in which people experience it, are afflicted by it, or conduct themselves in it. We do this, for example, when we define it in terms of space and time. This gives us what we call objective knowledge, and we contrast it with subjective vision, which is significantly colored by the experiencing subject. Science always aims at objective knowledge of the world, even though it ultimately has to admit that the observer is always a part of the picture. And scientists would still keep looking for objective knowledge even if it were shown beyond doubt that genuine knowledge—and particularly genuine knowledge of humankind—could never be attained by leaving out the human factor, but only by taking it, or, more accurately, the *whole human being,* in as well!

The objective view of life is transcended by the personal view—in other words, the objective view is only one of the views that a human being can take as a person. Its center of consciousness is the objectively defining ego—but this ego, too, is only one form of the subject. People who assume that this ego gives them an "absolute" standpoint turn everything it shows them into objects and combine these objects in a system that they then call the world. When they try to see that world objectively, they bend over backward to protect the "official" center of perception—the observing, defining, and classifying ego—against personal interference and distortion, desires, apprehensions, hopes, and anxieties—in short, against all emotions and urges. In effect, they erase themselves from the picture, throwing their own affections and afflictions overboard to make room for the objectively perceiving ego. What they are really trying to do is to reduce themselves to impersonal instruments of "objective knowledge." Like doctors dealing in "pure medicine," they would be only too happy to substitute an X-ray plate or test tube for themselves if they could. But can any "human being" pull this trick with his defining ego?

Personally perceived, the world orders and determines itself in relation to a subjective perceiver. Objective perceivers try to cancel this relationship, to eliminate themselves as "world's center." They invent an "objective consciousness," which all normal people supposedly acknowledge as part of their makeup, treat this as the center, relate everything to it, and rely on it for knowledge. Personally perceiving subjects, on the other hand, are automatically the center of the lives they live and the world they experience, and ultimately they determine the weight, value, meaning, and wider significance of both. The relative importance of the various items that make up the personal world reflects the concerns and priorities of the subject at its center. And when the subject is not centered, his or her world collapses into chaos. Conversely, a personal world of which fear or disorder is the keynote points to an uncentered subject.

When life is personally seen in this sense, there is nothing that does not point back to the perceiving subject. This is also why absolutely everything personally seen has, as it were, a *recognizable face.* Children, poets, and primitives are by no means the only ones to have the privilege of seeing the world like this. Even when we grow up and learn to see the world objectively, to perceive it rationally, and to ignore the mirror images and projections of the subjective self—our basic way of experiencing it is still the personal one. This helps us to understand why, in the personal vision of life, every object, every chair, house, stone, crack in the wall, cushion, teapot, tile, or cloud—and also every so-called abstract concept, such as hatred, justice, love, order—has a definite "face." Everything *meets* us, and everything we meet is a "being" that looks at us in a certain way, conveys a certain mood, and connects in a way that involves, attracts, or repels us. In this personal encounter with the world, all its qualities, associations, systems, and forms point inward to its center—the experiencing subject, who thus encounters *himself* at every turn. Provided that they do not shut themselves out of the picture, human beings see everything humanly, and automatically encounter themselves in everything they see.

Truth objectively sought is contaminated by the personal element (and so everything is done to eliminate its function as the center of knowledge), but discovering the human truth of life that is sought in the personal view depends on reading the meaning and significance of everything out of the perceiving subject and relating them back to that subject. Even the objective view and the things it registers are themselves comprised within the personal view, and so have their own "felt" qualities. Everything objectively perceived thus has a certain feeling of distance. There is something "cool" about it. Even the word *objective* has a certain emotional weight and its own color on the personal spectrum, and that which is "objectively determined" is also still experienced "personally."

When we listen to music we hear notes, rhythms, and melodies, not oscillations and abstract numerical series (even though series of this kind can be "objectively" identified, isolated, and even related in a certain sense to what we actually experience). Similarly, there is a yawning gulf between the things we actually see, taste, and touch, and the things that objective perception conceptualizes, measures, and presents to us in abstract, intellectual form. In fact, the world we experience is always a world charged with feeling, a world that is on our side or against us, that invites or rejects us, delights us or drives us to despair, fulfills us or leaves us empty and unsatisfied—and we experience all this as the counter-form of the form in which we experience ourselves and live ourselves out in that world. Ultimately, everything therefore depends on our life's focal point and our own state of mind and being, and this in turn depends on whether, and in what sense, we ourselves are centered. For this we ourselves are responsible.

Objectively, the term *center* denotes a middle point that can be spatially determined. Everything else "forms a circle" around this point, that is, in a certain sense orders itself around it. The middle, "inside" point is the center and source of order, and the surrounding area is its periphery—the "outside." The middle point is the center of the circle, and everything, when it moves, rotates around that center.

When we speak of the center in personal terms we are not speaking of the center of a system that can be spatially determined and measured. We still use all the concepts we use with spatial systems, but we give them a new and personal meaning. The "center" is now the focal point of a person's life and experience—and this is, above all, his or her own subjective self.

The personal subject is the center of his or her own world, and everything in that world has its roots, order, and significance in the personal subject. Each of us lives, loves, and suffers in his or her own world and personal reality; its priorities, substance, qualities, tensions, highs, lows, opportunities, perils, sense, and senselessness—all the components of its system and significance—unwaveringly reflect the form, attitudes, and life concerns of the subject who sustains it.

One distinction is vital on the way to the true self: that between the reality of natural ego and everyday personality, and the other reality that lies beyond the first and transcends it. These two realities are usually divided into human and superhuman, natural and supernatural, the world of earth and the world of heaven. The latter transcends the former and thus has a different status. We experience it as the realm that touches us in certain numinous qualities. Human beings are empowered and expected to distinguish between the two worlds and to dwell more in one than the other. Ultimately, however, they are also expected to unite the two within themselves. Both lie within the range of personal encounter. They spring from the twin roots of human life: world-ego and true nature!

The Three Basic Concerns of Humankind

Subjectively, we are our own world's center and the conscious or unwitting focus of everything around us, but this still does not tell us what it means to say that we ourselves are centered. Before we can answer the question "When are we centered?" we need to know something about the three basic and recurrent concerns of human life.

Our first concern as human beings is to *live*—simply to live and survive day by day. Anything that threatens this aim and endangers life, or even detracts from or makes it less safe, throws a shadow across our whole existence. Anxiety, apprehension, fear, and even terror take over, and we ourselves start to topple. As soon as life and survival are sure, anxiety fades and the danger passes, we recover our balance—swinging back, as it were, into our center. But what is "our center"? When there is nothing to disturb us, we feel centered. But is *feeling* centered really *being* centered?

Our second aim is not merely to live or survive, but to live *meaningfully*. Life seems meaningful when it clearly obeys our inner law and gives our existence a valid and harmonious shape. The components of this meaningful shape are order, justice, fulfillment, balance, and harmony—in repose and movement, in work and in leisure, in personal "form" and in a position and role in the world. When all of this seems safe, we feel that life is on an even keel; when it is lost, life becomes meaningless. Its harmony vanishes, and it becomes dull, empty, galling, absurd—and finally drives us to despair. Any disturbance of the system, any doubt that life can be meaningful, immediately sets the structures swaying; the world starts fissuring and threatens to collapse. The center that held it all together seems to have been plucked out.

The third aim has to do with *community*. Human beings are built for dialogue. They must have someone else to talk to. They cannot endure isolation. Even when they grow up, mature, become individuals, develop independent qualities, and leave their original community behind, they still seek company elsewhere. They need love, security, the shelter provided by an environing group. Without this they cannot really settle; knowingly or not, its presence becomes the one thing on which everything turns. Without it, life has no real center.

These three basic aims keep our lives on the move. Taken together, they also stand for the living center that animates us. They are the living root, the motive force and regulating principle of everything we do and do not do. When they are fulfilled, we feel balanced and more or less at ease (centered) and life seems in order. Any threat to fulfillment of any of them upsets the balance, fills us with alarm, and throws us into confusion. And yet even when all is well and we sometimes *feel* that we are at our own center, this still does not mean that we actually *are* there.

The Threefold Unity of Being as the Individual's Center

The three basic aims—to live, to live meaningfully, and to live as part of a community—express, in human terms, the triple unity of otherworldly Being: undivided *plenitude,* absolute *order* and all-embracing *unity.* At those times when Being is experienced—at turning points in life or increasingly as an adept advances on the inner Way—it reveals itself as Life in life, as the transcendent in the immanent, the otherworldly in the world, the absolute in the conditional, *true nature* in the self.

The threefold unity of Being appears in everything that lives—in plant, animal, and person—and always in true nature's language. More specifically, fullness is expressed in vital *strength,* order in the indwelling *law* and the innate Way to a definite *form,* and unity in vitalizing *wholeness,* which embraces everything and binds it together. Whenever Being is prevented from manifesting itself in existence, weakness and impotence take the place of strength, distortion and aberrance usurp true nature's form, and fragmentation and decay drive wholeness out. Conversely, Being's coming to fruition in a person is expressed in the vital joy of living, in the delighted creation or appreciation of meaningful form, and in the rapturous discovery of unity in love.

Whenever Being is unable to manifest itself, *fear, despair,* and *loneliness* take over. All this shows that *it is Being's ability and will to manifest itself in existence that is the secret center* around which all human life fundamentally revolves. This means that people are themselves truly centered only when the Absolute in their true nature can reveal itself in and through them as sustaining strength, meaningful form, and creative, redemptive love.

The vitalizing urge behind all human life is the manifestation of Being in existence, and fulfillment of this urge gives life permanence, meaning, and value; but the manifestation of Being is not just a vitalizing urge—it is also the individual's most sacred duty and deepest aspiration. The triunity of Being is venerated in the attributes of the divinity in all the world's religions. In Christianity it appears in the power, wisdom, and goodness of God the Father; in Buddhism, in the three treasures—Buddha, Dharma (the law), and Samgha (the community of the disciples); in Shintoism, in the three divine insignia—sword, mirror, and chain of precious stones.

This threefold unity is always the "highest" thing that humans revere in their images of God, but, because they have experienced this unity in themselves, it is also the "deepest" thing that comes home to them with absolute conviction and force in moments of grace: the incomprehensible fullness of otherworldly strength, meaning, and love inherent in their true nature. Their personal progress is reflected in changes in the level on which and conditions under which they can experience the signs of triune Being—strength, meaning, and security—finding their true center in them and living from it.

When *Life* comes to inner consciousness it speaks to us in a specific aspect of its threefold unity—redemptive or mandatory, liberating or subjugating, lifting us up or casting us down—but it always speaks as the inner master—that is, as inborn *Way*. To advance on that Way we need a new and broader consciousness that increasingly brings us the direct experience of Being and opens the way to total change. We cross the decisive threshold, beyond which the real center—Being itself—can come to consciousness as *our own* center, when we turn our back on ordinary consciousness, for which objective knowledge, technical proficiency, and fixed values and systems are the things that count. The static vision of ordinary consciousness runs counter to the dynamic of Being and, by reducing Life (Being) to an object, it makes us miss our true nature.

Three Kinds of Self-consciousness

The nature of a person's *self-consciousness* and the extent to which it is absolute or conditional show whether, and how far, he not only *feels* but *is* in his center. Self-consciousness again reflects the threefold unity of Being: it can mean consciousness of our own *strength,* consciousness of our own *value,* or consciousness of our *links with others.*

Consciousness of our own strength is the certainty that we are ultimately invincible. It is the feeling that we can face and overcome any danger—that somehow we will cope and win through. It is the firm belief that we have the strength to make up for any hurt, damage, or loss—however great—and to renew ourselves and put things right again. Once we have this sense of our own strength, every danger gives us an opportunity to test it—and is welcomed, rather than feared. Indeed, this bedrock conviction of our own strength is the very foundation of a life without fear.

Consciousness of our own value is the certainty that the world makes sense, that our own position in it is a meaningful part of a meaningful whole, and that our own value and the validity of our own existence are thus beyond doubt. Our faith is utter and positive, and despair cannot touch us.

Consciousness of our links with others is the certainty that we are safe in life's community, that we "belong." We never feel excluded, but are sure that we are loved—and sure that the love we feel for others is accepted and returned. It is the feeling that life is, by definition, a matter of living with others, and that this pattern has proved its worth universally. It gives us a radiant sense of being at one with ourselves and with the world around us. Our natural environment, and above all our human one, is a home and a haven in which our potential is effortlessly realized. We can be ourselves without shyness; we have a sense of being totally protected. The opposite of this is a situation in which we constantly wonder Do I belong? Am I loved? Are they going to throw me out?

We *feel* centered when our self-consciousness is, in these three respects, intact. Similarly, we feel alienated from our center when this is not the case. But to decide if we really *are* centered, we must take a closer look, always remembering that threefold self-consciousness can be present or absent on very different levels. In fact, there are at least three such levels: the first is naïve self-consciousness; the second is the self-consciousness generated by the worldly ego as long as it remains within its own horizons and relies on its own abilities; the third is the self-consciousness that comes when the self experiences Being and successfully fuses world-ego and true nature. Putting it another way: the first is the *child's* naïve, unfragmented self-consciousness; the second is the self-consciousness of *ego/personality,* and derives from the strength, talents, and skills needed to play a particular part in the world; the third is the self-consciousness that dawns when a human being becomes a window for the Absolute and thus, in the fullest sense, a *person.* We must learn to tell these three levels apart, and our ability to do so increases as we advance on the inner Way.

The Child's Self-consciousness

In its natural state, children's self-consciousness expresses a naïve confidence in themselves and in life—a confidence that is still intact, unthinking and secure from any outside threat. Its keynote is still a natural, *primal trust* in life's sustaining certainty. There is also an unquestioning *belief* that everything is as it should be, and that their own position is permanently and totally safe. Finally, there is a sense of absolute *security,* security expressed in the loving affection of others. At this stage, self-consciousness, world-consciousness, and life-consciousness are still the same thing. Primal trust, primal belief, and the primal sense of security together express a union with Being that is still complete. True nature has not yet been obstructed by world-ego. The child's life-consciousness survives intact until something unexpected flaws the primal bond or something terrible severs it entirely. These are the dramas of early childhood, and they typically occur when certain key figures shatter the instinctive, primal expectations of safety, meaning, and human warmth, which are the reflections of Being's threefold unity in the child's consciousness. The child's feeling for life is undivided, and this shows that the primal bond with Being is still more powerful in his or her consciousness than the world-feeling that the emergent ego is starting to generate—and still tips the scale in the relationship between that nascent ego and union with the Absolute. A person stays *in* his or her original center as long as this remains the case—and the inner core can even intercept and smooth over minor disturbances. Happy the man or woman who remains in close contact with the ground of Being as the world-ego develops.

The World-ego's Self-consciousness

As the world-ego develops, we increasingly come to stand on our own feet. We have to do this, and have to do it quickly, because early disappointments—always partly inevitable—have shattered our initial expectations and dimmed our original confidence, faith, and sense of security. From now on, our self-consciousness depends on learning to master life for ourselves. In this way, feeling safe, centered, and balanced stops depending on what we really are in our true nature—still-cherished children of Being—and becomes a matter of conscious reliance on the world-ego. At this stage, however, living and surviving depend very largely on "conditional" elements—circumstances, possessions, knowledge, and skills. As soon as the primal link with Being starts to fade from inner presence, all aspects of consciousness—not just consciousness of our own strength, but also consciousness of our own value and consciousness of ourselves in relation to others—come to depend on *worldly* conditions and on our ability to play the world's game successfully.

At the world-ego stage, *consciousness of our own strength* depends on what we *have, know,* or *can do.* Feeling balanced and in touch with our center is essentially a matter of feeling safe (that is, of feeling that we have the skills we need to cope and that our possessions and status are secure). The vital factors here may be health, money, position, superior knowledge and ability, or reliance on the people we live with. Feeling safe in this sense always means overcoming the dangerous and conditional elements in life. Coping is a question of having the right abilities or knowing the right people. If we have, or think we have, these abilities and connections, we feel safe. And this confidence allows us to feel—if only temporarily—that we are together and can now live from our center. But there is always the threat of something unexpected, always the possibility of sickness, always the ultimate certainty of death—and so the whole structure rests on sand. This is why we never entirely shake free of a secret unease and anxiety, a nameless fear. Never quite going away, this fear travels with us, giving the lie to our sense of being "centered." We do indeed feel that the door to our own center lies open when we know that our possessions, knowledge, and skills are more than equal to any challenge the world can bring us; but this "ability to live from our own center" is not absolute because it depends on certain worldly conditions. Admittedly once these conditions seem fulfilled we temporarily *feel* centered—but this still does not mean that we really *are* centered.

When the child's original confidence starts to fade at the world-ego stage, his *consciousness of his own value* (and the connected feeling that life and the world ultimately make sense) comes to depend on certain worldly conditions, and particularly on his ability to *grasp* the meaning of what is going on. The world we live in must in some way be "in tune," or at least not at odds, with our notions of justice and meaning. Here, too, our consciousness of our own value depends on being understood, acknowledged, and valued by the world. As soon as one of these conditions is lacking, uncertainty sets in, doubt undermines our sense of our own value, and we try to hold off feelings of inferiority by making an impression on others. In this situation our natural balance and serenity have been lost. We no longer rest within ourselves, we no longer feel centered, our self-consciousness has been disturbed. Once we turn into worldly "personalities" and sever our primal links with Being, any sense that our qualities are not being acknowledged, that we are not getting our due, disables us. We lose faith in meaning and justice, and this makes us lose touch with our center. In other words, we have a temporary feeling of being centered only when the world sees, values, and treats us in the way we deserve. The world being what it is, however, this kind of consciousness of our own value stands on shaky ground, and so we may well ask: *are* we ever really centered while our sense of ourselves and our belief in life depend on being acknowledged and grasping the meaning of everything?

As long as we remain the world-ego's prisoners, our *consciousness of belonging to a community* depends on the actual presence of another person or a sheltering group. Here, too—as in the case of consciousness of our own strength and consciousness of our own value—there is, of course, a naïve self-consciousness that nothing can shake or discourage. This is why certain people, whose roots in Being have survived into adulthood, are deeply, totally convinced that they are always welcome, always belong, and are universally popular. With a lack of tact that is positively touching, they bulldoze their way into even the tightest-knit group and demand intimacy where they have no right to expect it. But once the primal contact with Being has been lost, we no longer have this automatic sense of community. When we are alone, bereaved, or suddenly expelled from "our" community, life becomes impossible. Robbed of our center, we wander in a void, as if we had lost our own self. Conversely, when we have a warm and loving family, are happily married, or form part of a group in which trust, acceptance, and love are the norms—in other words, when "belonging" seems a fact of our existence—we feel that we can really be ourselves. We have a sense of being at the fulcrum of life, of being sheltered, and of being, as it were, affirmed at our own center. And, surrounded by the people who mean most to us, we feel that we have also reached our own center. But *are* we really centered? No, because the center we have reached is still conditional, still dependent on circumstance. Our true center must be unconditional, must show that we are anchored in the Absolute. When we are really "students on the Way," then fluctuations in self-consciousness become the inner master's voice, show us that we are going astray, and tell us to find another anchor for self-consciousness!

Self-consciousness from True Nature

We can also experience a *deeper self-consciousness*—self-consciousness from our *true nature*. Paradoxically, this affirms itself at the very point where everything that self-consciousness needs at the world-ego stage is missing or has been destroyed. It reveals itself chiefly in the three "Great Experiences" of Being, at the very moment when the normal foundations of life collapse beneath us. These are the experiences that bring us the sense of new *life* as death draws ineluctably nearer, of hidden *meaning* in the world's absurdity, and of deeper *security* in the midst of solitude—all of them lying beyond the world as we know it. These are the moments when Being enters inner consciousness—and this is why, when terror seems natural, we are filled with supernatural confidence; why, when the world's absurdity should drive us to despair, a new belief is born; and why, when ultimate loneliness should make life unbearable, we suddenly have an inexplicable sense of being sheltered and cherished. But what has really happened? What sage master's precept have we followed, knowingly or not? Quite simply, the wisdom that dares to accept annihilation and to sacrifice the security, meaning, and fellowship demanded by the world-ego. When this happens, the ego collapses at the limits of its strength and wisdom, and true nature is revealed! Experiences like this generate a deeper self-consciousness, a self-consciousness that has nothing to do with the things we can do, know, or face up to if certain conditions are fulfilled. There is a way of standing in otherworldly *strength in the midst of weakness*, experiencing otherworldly *clarity in the midst of the world's darkness*, and sensing the *sheltering presence of an incomprehensible love in the midst of the world's indifference*. It is only when something like this "enters our heart" that we touch our real center. In other words, this center is nothing more or less than true nature, faithfully affirming itself in here-and-now contingency—true nature in which timeless, absolute Being is present within us. Once special experiences like this have shown us the truth of Being in existence, then the center we have reached—at first hidden from us—can become the *conscious* center of everything we do. And, once the Way has taught us to hear the inner master's voice, any straying from that center can wake it. It is only at this point that everything in us can start to revolve, consciously, responsibly, and freely, around the unconscious center and purpose of all life—*manifestation of Being in the world.* In a human being this means, as he struggles, creates, and loves in constant contact with the Absolute, that his personal individuality becomes an ever-more-conscious witness to the fullness, order, and unity of Being. When he reaches his own center in this way, his deepest urge, his profoundest ethical imperative, and his transcendent longing come together in *one* movement that fulfills them all.

The Center: The Presence of Being in True Nature

Life's one, true, and real center—real because everything derives from it—is Being. Being contained and striving to manifest itself in every living form. Existence is multiple, and it reveals Being in an infinite variety of individual forms. The *inner form* of every contingent outer form is the innate *inner way,* the law of its life process, which it follows as it unfolds and fulfills itself in a specific series of stages and steps, finally passing out of being, but bearing new fruit in so doing—the seed of a further process of becoming. This inner way is the inborn and *operative* center of every living creature's existence. And so we, as conscious creatures, reach our true center only when this inner way is revealed to us as our own truth and moral law, when we become able to follow it, and when any departure from it wakes absolute conscience—that is, comes to awareness in the inner master's voice. In other words, we are centered only when we have finally started on the Way.

All living creatures unconsciously let the center of all life (and thus their own center) work in them, but humans have the power and the duty to do this consciously and to play a responsible part in giving it form. All living creatures live in Being, but humans have the power to live consciously from divine Being as their true center and to experience as conscience its urge to manifest itself in the world.

Consciousness of Being is far beyond the natural world-ego's reach, and awareness of Being's indwelling presence is by no means automatic. The experience of Being is, rather, a special kind of event, one that ego-world consciousness at first prevents from occurring. The manifestation of Being is our secret, basic concern as conscious beings, and it is anguish at separation from it that first fills us with longing and prepares us to experience its breakthrough into consciousness as something very special. When that breakthrough comes, it instantly, dramatically, frees us from ego-world consciousness. This obstructive consciousness can vary in nature and persistence, but it always generates tension, and resolution of this tension gives rise to another form of consciousness, in which Being can come a little closer to awareness and so show itself to us a little more clearly.

Any form of consciousness that stops Being from becoming manifest also stops us from reaching our true center. We do so only when we make room in our consciousness for Being to reveal itself.

The Way to the Center

If it is true that the state of being genuinely centered is a state that allows *transcendent Being* to manifest itself progressively in *consciousness*, then the way to this state is the *Way of initiation and individuation*. It begins when a person experiences Being.

After that comes a step-by-step process of initiation, instruction, and absorption that leads through various preordained stages from the surface to the depths, from natural consciousness to the consciousness in which our true nature—supraworldly Being living within us—can manifest itself as experience and driving force. The threshold to this way is "conversion"—a radical change of direction. From that point on, Being—or, rather, its ability to infiltrate our consciousness and turn us, step by step, into a personal medium for manifestation of itself—becomes the only thing that really counts. When it enters our existence—when superhuman true nature enters the human self—it frees us, imposes lasting obligations on us, repeatedly demands a kind of dying, and promises ultimate fulfillment, provided that we find and recognize our center in the neverending *process* of change. Conversion is effected in three ways: experience, insight, and practice.

The Way begins with the initiation experience—usually a lightning flash of revelation that transfigures everything. It is as if a dense fog had suddenly lifted to reveal a new center, a new meaning, and the promise of a new fullness, order, and unity. Mountains collapse, hidden chasms yawn, streams swell to fructifying torrents, and a new light dawns, like the sun blazing out as the moon fades away. These experiences are vital turning points. Their intensity, duration, and quality vary. They sometimes take us unawares in the midst of our daily routine, and they sometimes come when we are plunged in misery. Always, however, they have an absolute quality that carries immediate conviction. This is experience that has nothing in common with any natural experience—even allowing for what we already know about the "other dimension."

These experiences, which we call "experiences of Being," also generate self-consciousness from Being. We enter the Way when we start to take them seriously. They are not necessarily shattering experiences of the kind we sometimes have when our natural ego-world structure collapses at the outer limits of its strength.

Indeed, the experience of Being can come as an unexpected gift in the midst of "everyday life." While it lasts, the recipient is in a very special state, and temporarily centered as well. The way to the center opens when one's senses become sharp enough to register these initiation moments, at which true nature temporarily takes over. At times like this, everything one is, does, and experiences has a very special character. One's feeling for everything that helps one advance toward mediumship or prevents one from doing so is preternaturally heightened, and one's inner senses start to operate. It is as if one had previously been deaf and blind to Being. One can suddenly see into and hear one's own inner nature and the inner nature of everything around one—can, in other words, hear the master's voice.

In this case, being correctly *centered* means being centered on this kind of mediumship, focused on whatever may be shining through. This state is not fixed and static. It is, rather, a state of being-in-balance, of being-in-movement—movement that barely touches the ground, and being that consists of advancing without stopping, as if on a tightrope, where any pause could make us plummet. Every hesitation wakes the inner voice.

Being centered means being *open* in a special way, so that the spirit of Life can enter and leave without hindrance—but also closed in such a way that nothing vital is lost. The underlying concept here is that of living, ever-changing *form* as Life's medium and receptacle—a vessel that is felt to be precious and thus instinctively treated with care. In all of this there is *contact* with an inexpressible, intangible something maintained against all obstacles; we can keep it only by possessing it as if we did not possess it. These new ways of being open, having form, and being in contact are no mere passing privilege, but the stuff of a new code. The inner master wakes whenever we fail to respect that code.

Being centered is also a special way of being *awake,* with all our senses heightened and turned inward in a kind of brightening twilight in which everything glows from within. This, the "indwelling presence of Being," is a unique experience in which our separate senses—hearing, smell, taste, touch, and even sight—seem to grow back together and to blend in a new and special inner perception. None of them acts on or determines anything. Each is a receptor only, and each reflects without "possessing." This is why the whole state is also shot through with a special radiance that provides an inner light and also a vitalizing, nourishing warmth. Everything depends, however, on holding a mysterious balance—on heading in a certain direction and staying on a certain level, as if guided by a hidden master's hand. At this point we are mysteriously both the compass and what the compass points to—both the target and the instrument that registers every hairbreadth deviation from it. This is a sign that we are genuinely on the Way to our true center. For "being truly centered" is characterized by the fact that the person who has reached this center and the person who is repeatedly seeking, missing, and seeking it again are *one and the same.* This indescribable state—grace and the moment illuminated by it—is always temporary; for no one outruns his natural consciousness. But it can become the permanent ground of everything we experience if we persevere on the way to our real center and so gradually perfect ourselves as mediums.

Experiencing Being and being transformed from it are two different things. * Experience is not enough—insight and practice must follow if contact with Being and experience of it are to re-make a person. Being shown the light is one thing—seeing it is another.

The first step to knowledge is to see that the experience of Being is the starting point of a process of change that requires a lifetime's work. This insight is essentially the realization that foreground or "natural" consciousness is in fact the darkness of which St. John says that it "comprehends not the light." Rational consciousness reduces everything to objects and creates a static order. Both are incompatible with

*Cf. Karlfried Graf Dürckheim, *Erlebnis und Wandlung* (Bern/Munich: O. W. Barth-Verlag, 1982).

transcendent *Life,* which is supra-human and dynamic; they prevent it from revealing itself in human life. For thousands of years the wisdom of the East has been telling us that narrow, natural (merely objective) consciousness cuts us off from Being. It is time that we Westerners took this lesson to heart and realized that the only way of reaching our true center is to break through the limitations of objective consciousness.

There is, however, a second barrier, beyond *static ego-world consciousness,* that prevents our true nature from revealing itself and thus seals off our true center—the *shadow.*

The shadow is one of the most fruitful concepts of Jungian psychology. It stands for everything that we reject or repress—both primal life impulses and repressed life reactions to the wicked world. It is light in the form of the thing that obstructs it! We must look behind the shadow to its recurrent cause—to what really screens out true nature's light. The size and depth of the shadow give us the measure of the obstacle we face on the path to our true center; they also give us an idea of the limitless space that opens in front of us once we have mastered it. Learning what the shadow is, why it is there, and how we can overcome both it and the blocks that cause it is the central element in the *depth psychology* approach to clearing the Way. For our first contact with Being does not necessarily mean that the ground has also been cleared in the depth-psychological sense. To become a full part of the higher dimension and share in its pattern of never-rending change, we must repeatedly turn our back on what we are at any given time and admit the unknown side of our true nature—the principle of creative chaos within us. Our task is to prepare the ground in which the seed of Being can flower in what we experience, and ultimately in what we are, without being instantly choked by covert mechanism, undisciplined desires, precocious longings, and illicit attempts to seize the supreme good without the necessary maturity. It is no easy undertaking.

To prepare the way in depth psychology, we must also

know about the sequence of steps that leads to transformation of the self. "Allowing the reality that lies behind wrong up-bringing or unconsciousness to make itself felt is the basic rule, beginning, and aim of all our work. As wrong forms are seen for what they are and dismantled, new elements can always be expected to emerge from the background, and the underlying creativity and shaping energy to wake."* This kind of conversion depends on rejection of the old order, on destruction of the old subjective stance, on death of the ego, and on genuine surrender of the old form—the sacrifice without which any change is impossible. Nor, unless we are willing to make this sacrifice, can we ever reach our center.

Transformation is a complex process, and people who are being transformed must experience, suffer, and live the great forces that confront each other in them—light and darkness, male and female, rich and poor, height and depth, life and death—both as relatively separate and as antithetical principles, before the opposites coincide in the real experience of change and are resolved in the experience of *light* beyond light and darkness. This supreme experience is the first, shattering encounter with the true center. But the *experience* of supra-antithetical Being, which demands neverending change, as the true center is still a long way from the *state of mind and being* in which, having truly matured, we continue without stopping on the Way to total change, achieve union with our center, and live from it. This is a Way on which we never arrive—a Way that is itself the goal. In fact, we reach our center at the very moment when we finally reach the Way that leads to it.

But becoming centered in this way is by no means the end of suffering. On the contrary: it is only when we open up, let the other dimension in, see it as the indestructible root of our own being, recognize that we have a duty to it, and accept that duty utterly, that we can accept suffering. Indeed, one of the signs that we have reached our center is that we *can* suffer,

*Maria Hippius, "Am Faden von Zeit und Ewigkeit," in *Transzendenz als Erfahrung,* ed. M. Hippius (Weilheim: O. W. Barth-Verlag 1966), p. 29.

not that we stop suffering! To overcome suffering in our true nature means *being able* to suffer to the end, suffer until suffering ceases to be suffering. This victory over suffering first tempers the form that witnesses reliably to Being in the world. Anyone who has really tasted Being naturally feels the urge to lose himself in its redeeming presence and turn his back on the world. But failing to hazard the brightness of contact with Being in repeated confrontation with the dark forces of life is the surest way of losing it. Risking everything is the only way of attaining the form that allows us to maintain contact with our true nature consciously, responsibly, and freely, and so remain centered—not temporarily but permanently. Humans who attain their supreme form are still human. Reaching our true nature "outside the world" still leaves us wide of our personal center, and we find it only by bringing true nature and world together again. The key to this, however, is systematic exercise.

Also vital in preparing for the revelation of Being in existence and thus for the state of being centered is *practice*—exercises that involve working on the right way, not only of living *inwardly* but of being *in the world*. This always includes a disciplined effort to make the *body* right. "This is the only way in which the impulse toward wholeness and toward the building of a comprehensive consciousness can legitimately realize itself in the here-and-now. In the cosmic sense, the body is also the matrix in which all the spiritual elements can be absorbed, remake themselves as essentials, take on form, and become productive. The physical embodiment of insight is quite as necessary to the healthy development of the spiritual person as the kindling of the spirit's 'sacred fire,' that irradiates dull materiality and first gives it life."* Working on the body is central to the Way as practice toward fulfillment. Of course, the body we are speaking of here is not the body in contrast to mind and soul—not the body we have, but the body we *are*.

*Hippius, "Am Faden von Zeit," p. 32.

The Center in the Body's Symbolism

Being centered is totally expressed in the body—in right posture, in the constantly shifting and constantly remade balance of the whole, in consonance with our true nature, and in the harmonious movement that reflects it. This harmony, which is the outer sign of mediumship, is not static and has nothing to do with measure and proportion—it is a dynamic state, and it ensures that there is nothing left in the body to prevent Being from manifesting itself as movement and change. Indeed, we are physically centered only when the basic movement of life—the rhythm of creation and redemption, emergence and dissolution, opening and closing, giving and recovery of the self, in short, the "breath of life"—is written into our body, and anything that obstructs, restricts, or distorts Life's transforming movement is instantly detected and corrected to let it shine through.

"The body's symbolism helps us to grasp 'man's position in the cosmos' (Scheler) in a palpable sense. The symbolic disposition of the body and its members also provides a starting point for the analyst of the human form when he sets out to interpret humanity's true nature morphologically."* The meaning of the body and of external bodily form primarily lies in the body's function as the medium through which we live ourselves out physically in a process of neverending change. Its symbolism is not an abstract system projected onto an impersonal, independent body—because no such body actually exists. In fact, the symbolic significance of the human body and its various components and functions can be grasped only by seeing it as the mode in which individuals live themselves out, "have" themselves, are there, stand for something, and progressively find or fail to find the outer form demanded by their own innate law. This is also why the terms *upper* and *lower* essentially have a personal, rather than a physical, meaning when used of the body. "The secret symbolism of the contrast

*A. Vetter, *Personale Anthropologie: Aufriss der humanen Struktur* (Munich/Freiburg: Alber, 1966), p. 16.

between the vertical axis, in which human beings stand, and the horizontal plane, on which they walk (and which they share with the land animals), is incomparably suggestive when we set out to intuit the meaning of the human form."* "Upper" and "lower" denote relationships between dimensions, orientations, and states of human life, and their meaning in terms of the whole person repeatedly points to essential stages on the path to mediumship. "Upper" refers, for example, to the possibility of raising oneself and overcoming something "lower" that pulls one down. Heavy and light, hard and soft, solid and fluid—all these definite qualities have no "real" meaning of their own, but refer primarily to human experience and ways in which human beings can develop, move, and fulfill themselves. It is only when they are defined, objectivized, classified, and treated as abstractions that they become the fixed qualities and concepts of a material reality that supposedly exists "in itself."

This is why the significance of parts of the body also varies as an individual develops; at one point in the process they can be stages and at another foci—sometimes base and sometimes center. In certain circumstances, the earth (the ground on which we stand) is experienced as our base. In others, the abdomen, with all that it suggests and signifies, may be registered as base. The word *base* means one thing when we use it of the ground and another when we apply it to the transforming matrix centered in the pelvis, to which we must open ourselves and into which we must repeatedly descend on the Way of change if we are not to harden and grow sterile in the *upper* region—head (thought), chest (will), and heart (feeling).

When we focus on our links with the cosmic forces, we experience the area below the navel, the abdomen, as our center. But if we focus on the constant up-and-down movement between heaven and earth, which brings us to personhood, then the abdomen, as the source and sphere of the root

*Ibid., p. 14.

forces that sustain and renew us, is the base, while the head is not merely the part closest to heaven (in contrast to the feet) but also the mental sphere. And in this scheme of things the center is no longer the abdomen but the *heart.* The heart lies midway between heaven and earth, and something totally new can emerge in the upper/lower tension of which it is the focal point.

Discovering our "vital center" (or earth-center),* which is physically located in abdomen and pelvis, is decisive on the way to becoming a medium. It constitutes the first step on the way from world-ego to person.

Generally speaking, we are not on the way to mediumship, and thus our own center, until we have experienced, recognized, and begun to practice resting calmly in the body's center as the precondition of the right relaxed state and the right form. Admittedly, Westerners are at first surprised, if not shocked, when they hear that the belly (or, more accurately, the abdomen and pelvis) is the first center they must establish and maintain to make the body, too, a medium for Being. But first impressions are deceptive, and the "seat" we mentioned earlier actually holds, *in* the body, the secret of exercise aimed at the whole person's center.

The belly is frequently emphasized in romanesque and early gothic representations of the human figure (and also in images of Christ as Lord of the World), and has long been regarded as important in the East, and particularly Japan, where it is accepted as a vital element in exercising toward maturity, toward integration with the Absolute. In Japan, this is expressed in the doctrine and practice of *Hara.*

Literally, *Hara* means "belly." Metaphorically, it denotes a general state of mind and being that frees us progressively from the puny ego and anchors us calmly in a reality that gives us a new feeling for life and mastery of the world, and enables us to give ourselves entirely to fulfilling our true purpose in the world—to fight, die, create, and love

*Cf. Dürckheim, *Hara*.

without fear. Once we successfully settle and anchor ourselves in *Hara,* we experience it as the seat of life forces with which we are vitally connected and that can dispassionately absorb, melt down, and reshape all the ego's hardened forms. This discovered capacity for change and renewal also means that we can take the world differently. Nothing upsets us, nothing disturbs our dynamic equilibrium. Our head stays cool, our whole body is relaxed yet alert, and our breathing follows the rhythm of opening and closing, giving and re-finding of the self—the center's breathing rhythm. In the midst of the world's tumult, we preserve our serenity. In *Hara,* we rest in the source of inexhaustible energy and neverending change, and thus in the sphere where our personal process of being and becoming has its roots. The *Hara-no-hito,* or "person with belly," is someone who has reached maturity—who has created the conditions in which world-ego and true nature can merge. Lowering ourselves from the ego sphere into the *Hara* sphere (the earth-center), and anchoring ourselves in it, is ultimately the only way of achieving balance and reaching our own center. Once we understand the practice of *Hara,* we hear the master's voice in our body as soon as we fall, or are on the point of falling, out of our physical center—for example, when we are in danger. It is precisely in moments of danger that the uncentered, ego-ruled person tends to "pull himself up" and go rigid.

But we can "have *Hara* " and "be in *Hara* " and still not *be* centered. *Hara* is still not the *personal* center. Reaching the earth-center is not enough—we must also connect firmly with the heaven-center.

The heaven-center is on a different plane. Reaching it means contacting the forces of the spirit. The earth-center must be kept open, however, if a person is to receive the seed of the spirit (Logos) without confining it in logical systems and thus distorting it.

In body symbolism, the earth-center is located in the abdominal and pelvic region, the natural matrix that links us with the forces of the cosmos, while the heaven-center is located higher up—not actually in the head, but around the head and also in the chest-neck-head complex and its aura.

The world-ego's prism reduces the "lower" superhuman forces—the overflowing cosmic energy, in which we all share to start with—to mere images and concepts of sensual urges and needs, and it also reduces spirit, in the sense of Logos, to logical, ethical, and aesthetic systems. Of course, the world-ego's "values" are the mode in which Being is perceived in that prism, but they are also corrupted by the world-ego's tendency to define and pin things down—process them into static, traditional, petrified systems that finally cut us off from Being. These fixed systems must also be dissolved in the earth-center if we are to be free to receive Being's vital impulse, which transcends all fixities and allows the higher center, the *heaven-center,* to emerge.

Basically, the heaven-center is Being, which space/time contingency does not and cannot touch—in other words, the source of those *experiences* of Being in which we encounter the *Absolute* beyond space and time, *Life* beyond the reach of death, *meaning* purged of all unmeaning, and *love* transcending all the world's indifference.

When we experience this heaven-center in ourselves and remain in it, we leave the world behind. When we are in this state, and totally filled with our true nature, we may briefly *feel* centered in it. But because we are human and inescapably linked to the body, as we are to space and time, we *are* not truly centered as long as we rest in true nature alone—although the moments when true nature totally fills and sustains us give us a foretaste of what *being* truly centered means.

Only when heaven and earth are reconciled and fused do we reach our true center. This center—again in terms of body symbolism—is the *heart.* It is the opening of the heart that brings us children of heaven and earth to our true center.

This means that sharing in the earthly (cosmic) and heavenly (spiritual) powers that transcend the world-ego is still not enough to make a human being a person. On the contrary, sharing in these forces is not personal—either in the ordinary sense or in the special sense that concerns us here. The forces of the earth are pre-personal, those of the spirit supra-personal. We can all go beyond the natural ego, enter both these realms, and work from them—and still not be persons in the fullest sense, still not do what we do as persons. The forces of earth and spirit may hold us in their grip; their alternating pattern may absorb our ordinary ego so totally that we live and work as if it no longer existed, and not just when inspiration and enthusiasm lift us up and drive us on, but also in our responsible daily activities (for example, as healer or pastor). What we do may be highly valuable, but we still fail to give ourselves completely in doing it. We ourselves, as unique individuals, real only in the thousand contingencies of a particular body, a particular destiny, and particular joys, sorrows, hopes, and fears—in a word, we ourselves as a particular *human being*—are still not really present in what we do, and this makes it incomplete. Every true teacher, doctor, therapist, and indeed, pastor, knows that his relationship with pupil, patient, or seeker-after-help changes dramatically when he is suddenly driven to open himself entirely, step through his official function, and confront the other as the person he really, totally is. The dangers are many, but he knows deep down that he is now getting through as person to person for the first time.* Of course, this is really beneficial only when the giver and guide has himself reached his personal center. The breakthrough to genuine personal commitment is easily missed if the giver has, as it were, shed his self in allying himself with the cosmic or the spiritual forces. He lives, loves, creates, and operates from his earth-center or his heaven-center, but still not from the center of his personal "being-in-the-world." What he does may be useful, but he does it pre-personally, like many healers, or non-personally, like many priests. "The human being seen as a whole, that is, in the

*Cf. H. Trüb, in *Heilung aus der Begegnung* (Stuttgart: Klett, 1951).

round, is not just a link between earth and heaven, between nature and spirit, and both himself by turns—but the fusion of the two in an enlightened consciousness."*

"The person is the central connecting link that the human structure needs, and without which it would be something merely thought, and not real. . . . In body symbolism, the numinous person is located at the point where spirit and body, upper and lower, intersect."†

And so the personal center is not what *Hara* embodies, or the upper realm represents, but the *heart*! This is not the heart as seat of the positive and negative emotions that bind us to the world—but the heart that opens only when we have left everything behind at the ego stage, have plumbed the earth, scaled the heavens, and finally discovered the point that connects them both *in ourselves*. This is the great heart, the heart venerated by Christians as the heart of Jesus—it is no mere chance that Christian iconography places it at the center of the body, close to the solar plexus. *This* is the heart we mean when we speak of the heart as our personal center.

The Heart—
The Center of the Cross

The *heart of the center* alludes to our double status as children of heaven and of earth. But this heart does not open and we do not reach our center until our experience of the Absolute is no longer intermittent—the product of emotional surges—but when we children of heaven and earth have become reliable witnesses to Being, which transcends them both. But let us ask again what we mean by "heaven" and "earth."

"Earth" implies the maternal and cosmic forces of nature as against the paternal forces of word and spirit implied by "heaven." But this antithesis is not simply a way of distin-

*Lama Anagarika Govinda, "Durchbruch zur Transzendenz," in *Transzendenz als Erfahrung.* p. 270.
†Vetter, *Personale Anthropologie.* p. 18.

guishing the impersonal forces of nature from the universal and equally impersonal forces of the spirit, in whose archetypes, principles, laws, and systems we and all living creatures have a share. The heaven/earth antithesis is actively implanted within us as the Yang and Yin rhythm—the eternally creative process in which Life goes out of itself, loses and fulfills itself in individual forms, and returns redemptively home to the great All-One.

"Earth" is also, however, *Life* become contingent—here-and-now life, individually lived in particular circumstances, fulfilling a particular destiny, subject to the inevitable limitations of vulnerability, old age, and death, and filled with its own particular sufferings. "Heaven," by contrast, is universal Being, beyond the reach of fate, eternally young, and outside space and time—Being to which, as Eastern wisdom teaches, a person can "wake" as his or her "Buddha-nature" from the bonds of the ego-world illusion. When we look into the eyes of someone who is really on the way to wholeness, however, what we see is not merely world-ego contending with its own destiny, or true nature concealed behind that ego and beyond the reach of fate, but a personal ego—an ego located at the intersection of the timeless verticals and time-bound horizontals, at the center of that tension, compounded of longing, promise, and suffering, that characterizes the everlasting struggle to bring heaven and earth, true nature and world-ego, absolute Being and contingent existence together in the right way. It is only in this tension's energy field that a person's true center is formed, and only in that center that he or she reaches wholeness. It is only from that center that the *heart of the center* opens—the heart whose love is neither the vital but impersonal warmth of the cosmos, nor the bloodless, intellectual love of a "heaven-center" that either knows nothing of the earth or rejects it. The personal center in the true sense opens only when heaven and earth are united. It is revelation of the Absolute *in* the contingent—strength in weakness, sense in absurdity, love in the world's cruelty—that brings us to our true center, where we are conscious of being united, in the world, with something beyond it. Here we know that we must live toward, in, and from that dimension, and find in that knowledge the strength to accept that we are bound, as creatures of the world, to betray it again and again by sacrificing the eternal (vertical) to the temporal (horizontal). Ultimately, this means that being *personally centered* is not a matter of finally reaching a fixed point but of faithfully and calmly accepting the situation symbolized by the cross, and cooperating uncomplainingly with an everlasting to-and-fro movement in which we live and work from the world to the center and back again. In this movement, absolute spirit repeatedly takes on here-and-now form, "losing itself" in multifarious contingency, which must then become transparent so that heaven's light can shine purely from it. And so it is only when living out this conflict of intersecting forces (the cross) becomes the determining factor that a human being is really there, as a person, at his or her center. This center is thus the Absolute, driving on toward self-manifestation in the individual, but revealing itself in the human world only in the form of the cross.

When individual people find this center—become, in other words, windows for the Absolute—their experience acquires a special radiance; they themselves emit a special light, and everything they do, everyone they meet, also becomes a window for the Absolute. For, with a kind of gentle force, they center everything and everyone on their path.

We are centered when we live *in* the world from otherworldly true nature. Our true nature makes us share in divine Being, but this sharing becomes conscious as experience, obligation, and fulfillment only if we also accept ourselves as what we uniquely, contingently are. When we experience ourselves absolutely in our true nature as Being's special mode, we do so *in* contingency, not in spite of it. And it is precisely by affirming our own contingency that we may be given the *grace* to sense universal true nature in our individual true nature, to experience ourselves united in faith with the source of all form, with

Christ as "Word." This really obliges us to say that we are centered when we know ourselves united with Christ, live from Christ, and are repeatedly summoned back to this center by the inner master, whom we call Christ—not simply as the "true nature of everything that is," not simply as the innate law of becoming from true nature, but as that otherworldly authority that stands for and demands union with the contingent. Because we are anchored in the world, we are never completely united with our true nature, and our only *experience* of union with it comes in the form of a vital *encounter.* In this encounter, and provided that we experience ourselves *personally* at the agonizing point where heaven and earth intersect, Christ appears to us, not as a principle, but as a divine *You.*

The inner eye of personhood does not open until we experience ourselves in relation to the cross, the point of intersection. And we are not personally centered until the eye that is spiritually, essentially "of the sun" has opened—the eye we may term the Christ-eye, in which the person who sees becomes one with the person who sees him or her. Strictly speaking, this eye is no longer the normal human eye, and the center it shows us is no longer the center of an "external" life lived entirely from the ego, or an "internal" life lived completely from true nature—but the center of the life we live as the person we remain when world-ego and true nature are fused, at the point where "inner" and "outer" meet and intersect. In experiencing ourselves as focused on the point of intersection (the cross), we might even be said to enter into dialogue with Christ. The personal, divine "You" reveals itself in us as humanity's innermost ground. In experiencing ourselves to the end, we experience personal dialogue with God, and thus with our divine partner, as the deepest thing there is—and this divine partner, who is our real inner master, repeatedly drives us back to this experience.

We can thus say that a person is centered when he or she is in Christ. One hesitates to make this kind of statement because it easily loses its force when serenely accepted by people for whom it is an article of faith and not a matter of experience and total change—not, as we mean it here, the infinite goal of a Way that leads through death and transformation.

The Way of initiation is prefigured and transcended by *faith*—provided that faith is not simply the easy assumption that certain things are true, but is an expression of the Absolute coming to life in a person's inner nature. In this sense, we are centered at every stage in our inner development—and centered, depending on our maturity, in our own special way. The way of initiation is not meant for everyone. But some people are meant to experience Being in the ways possible *for them*, to learn from those experiences, and, as an ongoing process of individuation pushes back the natural limits of consciousness, to become consciously what they are fundamentally—children of heaven and earth—and witness to it. Even for people like these, the experience of the Absolute that makes them feel safe and floods their hearts with peace—the ultimate stage that a "simple soul" can reach—can become a threat, can turn negative in the temptation to stand still and thus throw everything away. At the very moment when they believe they have reached their center, they lose it again because they stop moving! But then, if their call is a true one, the master's voice startles them into realization and throws them onto the road to further change.

The Voice of the Master in the Encounter with Death

The master speaks to us when we find ourselves facing up to death. He speaks to us as the voice of that Life of which the death of all life forms a part and that makes dying the precondition of becoming.

Death is a part of life, as is suffering—indeed, life, suffering, and death are all inextricably entwined. Suffering can make us bitter or mature, depending on whether we experience ourselves only as natural egos, for whom pain-free survival is still the goal and target, or know ourselves grounded in supernatural true nature and see its progressive revelation of itself as the meaning of life. In the latter case, suffering removes all the obstacles to growth from our true nature. The natural ego, on the other hand, sees suffering and death as the dark sides of life—*the shadow.* But what is a shadow if not light in the form of the thing that obstructs it? When someone becomes a transparent medium for *Life* that lies beyond living and dying in the normal sense, the shadow vanishes, and Life appears in the form of our true nature, which cannot be realized as long as the world-ego, with its rooted aversion to all dying, holds sway.

Multiplicity is the law of our existence, and the fullness of Being cannot open up within us until it ceases to operate. Multiplicity resounds within and around us, and the voice of our true nature can only be heard when it falls silent. This is why spiritual exercise aims at stillness, in which sounds, thoughts, and images are entirely poured away, so that something that lies beyond them all can enter and take possession of us.

When multiplicity vanishes, the *One* can appear. When multiplicity falls silent, fullness can speak; when multiplicity dies, the One can live.

This is what the master's voice tells his students, reminding them of the *One* concealed within them whenever multiplicity threatens to engulf them.

In ancient Japan, many a Zen master saw death as his guide on the path to all-resolving Being and went out to meet it in a very special way. When he sensed that his time had come, he invited his friends to share a last meal with him. Afterward, he took his place in the center of the circle, wrote out a last poem, and sank into a deep reverie—from which he never awoke.

A dead person's face is stony and impenetrable—it seems incredible that where there was life just a moment ago there is suddenly absolute stillness. But if we look calmly at that face and stay quietly and receptively beside the dead person, we may feel the breath of the wholly different *Life* into which he or she has just entered. And suddenly we may also hear—from a long way off and yet just beside us—a voice that throws open a wholly new dimension.

Death brings fear into the world, and the primal human being instinctively runs in terror from the incomprehensible mystery that confronts him in its presence. This reaction is, in fact, a common one—we all know the terror that a dead body inspires. The way from this first, instinctive panic to looking death calmly in the face is a long one, and enduring death's silence is the first step. Death commands silence, and its stillness at first reduces everything around it to silence. Silently enduring this silence is the only way of coming sufficiently close for it to start speaking. Death speaks only to those who are silent before its mystery and still in its presence. Only people who can listen quietly will hear the Great Master's voice when they find themselves face to face with death.

A person dies. The pulse stops. The eyes grow dim. The breathing ceases. Unfathomable silence. A corpse? Not yet, for true nature's hour has come—and the hidden now reveals itself. When the last struggle is over, a door seems to open deep inside—the door behind which true nature has been waiting all that person's life. Bursting out, it now floods the still responsive substance of the face, changing it utterly, and giving it the look that has been called the radiance of death.

A mysterious middle state separates dying and being dead. This can sometimes be seen in a special glow that comes immediately after death. It expresses two things: redemption from one element and liberation into another—inner certainty and radiant serenity.

It is natural that grief at the death of a loved one should at first be stronger than happy memories of a shared past. Gradually, comfortingly, and fruitfully, however, the deepest element in the relationship—the presence of the Absolute within it—can then start to enter inner consciousness. Present in absence, the loved one's reassuring and yet challenging voice speaks to us in the language of Life, which remakes both the living and the dead in its own image.

We start dying the moment we are born. Death is woven into life, and everything that lives and grows lives toward its own death and from the death of the things it outgrows. This is all part of an unconscious, everlasting, and painless process of change. The growth of the ego that determines, holds fast, and circles fixed points makes it harder, however, to move on and make room for the new. Happy the man or woman who knows how to leave things behind! But one day death in the real sense approaches. This is something more than the dying involved in every change. It means growing through and beyond this literal dying—the ultimate growing-beyond-self.

Far sooner than we like to think, death—painless as a slowly spreading cancer—starts calling and gathering us to itself. But what is this death? Surely it is the gateway to a greater Life beyond, and surely true maturity should enable us to open ourselves to this greater life when we die? Those who are merely concerned with prolonging their lives as they grow older, who never stop to consider what longer life would bring them, are missing Life's ultimate purpose. Some people are convinced that dying well is more important than living longer—and indeed, no one can live well unless he or she also dies well.

Sometimes the imminence of death makes us ask ourselves deep down: Is it really death—or is it the power of *Life* that breaks out when the gates of death open—that frightens you?

People on the way to true maturity may suspect, and then increasingly know, that everything that seems to protect, sustain, and preserve them in this life is also a threat, because it forms a barrier to growth. The preserving forces of life are always accompanied by the petrifying forces of death—but the servants and messengers of Life are always the companions of destruction.

Mother earth casts out the children she has carried and nurtured, only to reabsorb them at a later stage. Is this a once-only happening? By no means; for humans, who are born to be free, must repeatedly succumb, on their way to that freedom, to the irresistible force that draws them back to the great mother before, finally and freely united with her and charged with her energy, they have the strength to destroy her in themselves and so break through to independence.

What death means for us depends on what we understand by "life." Since death's face changes with the eyes that look at it, it is our own maturity and mentality that determine whether we see it as a threat to life, mercilessly cutting it short, or as something that is part of life and yet points beyond it to another life, in which the familiar yields to the unknown, or perhaps to an Absolute beyond time and change. Our view of death depends on the extent to which we have come to awareness of true nature, in which something timeless is striving to reveal itself both in time and beyond time.

We must distinguish between:

Fear of dying and the pain of dying;
Fear of the dead and of the unknown that confronts us in the dead; and
Fear of what comes after death.

These three types of fear are all destructive forces in anyone still ruled by the natural world-ego. Anyone who is on the *Way,* and who sees them as aspects of the self that must be left behind, hears in them the master's warning voice, enjoining obedience to true nature's law of change.

Three kinds of death can be died:
Death of old age and disease;
Death in the service of a cause;
Death as the bridge-toll to the further shore.

All die the first;
Many are prepared to die the second;
But the third is open only to those few
In whom death of this life already lives
As experience, promise, and inner law.

Death is a part of life—but life is also a part of death. There are peoples who do not speak of "life and death" as we do—but of "life and rebirth." Life does not simply end with death, but also grows out of death—indeed, life always opens out into new life.

It is because of its close links with death that life is so enigmatic and mysterious. All the deep things it shows us are in some way connected with the death that awaits us. It is only the presence of death that allows us to experience the fullness of life in this world, and gives us a premonition of the fullness of supra-worldly *Life.* The depths remain closed as long as we refuse to face up to dying, give ourselves over to the world and its superficial pleasures, and live as if death did not exist. It is only when we know and confront death's acolytes—dread, fear, and terror—that we catch the glow of infinity that streams through the finite, transcends its limitations, carries us beyond it, and shows us eternity in it. This glow is a mere reflection of the light that we ourselves carry within us, and we see that light only when we become capable of looking death in the face and accepting it.

The general fear of growing old includes the fear of life's diminishing and of death's approaching. To the natural ego, youth is the time when the possibilities are infinite, while aging means the progressive narrowing-down of those possibilities. But age should bring maturity, and maturity always includes the ability to hear the inner master's voice. If we mature as we grow older, hear true nature's voice, and are focused on growing, then our future horizons are not narrowed by age, but extended. We are old when we have no future left, but maturing keeps us young, since growing old makes it steadily easier to leave nonessentials behind and focus on the one thing that matters: perfecting ourselves as a medium for the great Life within us as it drives toward manifestation of itself. The approach of death—to the natural ego, the ultimate terror—now appears as the consummation of our growing freedom to leave everything behind and enter freely into the limitless realms of the Great Unknown.

Death is the medium in which Life appears in the realm of living true nature on the threshold of every renewal. It is the ceasing-to-be on which every coming-into-being depends, and it lies at the heart of everything that is—as the promise of what it may become, and of emergence as new form. Becoming one thing necessarily involves ceasing to be another, and every birth implies a death. Those whose only interest is in permanence are cutting themselves off from *Life*—for they are denying Life's medium, death that makes room for it. . . . Once they have woken to the Way of change, however, they are ready to accept the thousand deaths that Life demands of them at every stage in their existence.

Human beings are tensioned between two poles: *absolute Life that lies beyond life and death,* and *contingent life that has a beginning and an end.* Personhood allows and obliges them to unite the two elements as aspiration, possibility, and duty. It is seeing how each can imperil the other that brings their significance home. Each has a purpose that finds fulfillment in the other. What is mortal life really meant to do? To witness in mortality to immortality! And what does immortality mean? Giving mortality a home in immortality! This first becomes a possibility when a person wakes to the Way, becomes a student, and hears the voice of the Master, in which Life repeatedly and bindingly comes to consciousness as task, conscience, and energy.

Being human means living as part of a community and

adjusting to an objectively ordered world. If the community swallows us, or that world objectivizes us, we run the risk of alienation—of losing contact with ourselves. But if we can still find, in the heart of our true nature, the strength to say no, a homeward-pointing light may suddenly shine out in the darkness, and the death that threatens us from loss of self may turn into a life of growing self-discovery. This is the vital theme of our own era!

As long as we live, death remains our constant companion. But until we realize that we are exiles, we misunderstand its presence and see it merely as the enemy of here-and-now life. It is only when we grasp the significance of those moments when we sense a new life beyond imminent death, or experience new birth beyond a kind of dying, that infinity reveals itself and we suspect, intuit, and finally know that death is not simply the end. Nearly everyone has had an experience like this at some point in his or her life—hardly anyone has learned how to hear Life's voice in death.

Children do not turn into adults until their parents "die"—stop shielding them and making decisions for them. Whenever a powerful father figure or mother image dominates the unconscious, a dream in which the child kills the parent may well herald independence. Dreams of this kind are often accompanied or followed by a sense of horror at the deed—but also by the knowledge that the deed itself is a necessary one. When he "kills" his parents in this way, the child is obeying the master's voice. Waking brings a sense of liberation—and with it love comes back. Indeed, real love—love based on freedom—is born for the first time.

One can die of hunger and one can also die of satiety. The saint still needs a physical minimum, while the sybarite retains some spark of spirituality. If that minimum is withdrawn, or that spark extinguished, death follows in both cases. And yet, it is the proximity of death that keeps both sybarites and saints alive—the first because they flee it, the second because they go to meet it.

The meaning of every death lies in the life it makes

possible. The indestructible shines out in destruction, and "bravery" means risking destruction to sense the indestructible behind it. It is only danger that allows us to glimpse something that no danger can touch. This is why some people risk their lives in the mountains, and others in combat, and why the brave have always gone fearlessly, chivalrously out and conquered death, sensing from the start the bright light of Life that flames up in it.

"Of course I'll do it again," said a woman who had tried to kill herself. "Why?" "Because it was such a wonderful feeling when I'd taken the poison, and had left myself and everything else behind as if I and it were nothing."

"A life that means survival has no meaning!" said a Jew on the point of being gassed. A moment before he had been trembling and terrified; now he was suddenly, radiantly calm—and fate passed him by.

There are three kinds of anguish that can kill: fear of annihilation, despair at life's absurdity, and utter loneliness. But when death seems unavoidable, new life can suddenly burst from all three: when we are given the grace to do something we could never ordinarily do—to accept the unacceptable. When we find the strength to face up to, accept, and submit to the inevitable of our own volition, we rob even death of its sting. Willingness to sacrifice the old ego opens the door to true nature, allowing it to enter the new, real, and personal self. And suddenly something indestructible emerges from destruction; a light beyond meaning and unmeaning dawns from dark despair at life's absurdity; and the sense of total worldly isolation yields to the sense of being sheltered in otherworldly Being.

Just as belief is not truly belief while doubt can still touch it,
just as freedom is not truly freedom while constraint can still limit it,
so Life is not truly Life while the thought of death can still disturb it.

True human progress—the progress that humanizes in the fullest sense—is not a matter of finding new ways of making life safer (that kind of security can actually mark a regression), but of increasing the strength that allows people to win an inner triumph over death. This only comes, however, from deepening experience of a greater Life that has nothing to do with the death died in time.

Fidelity to one's beliefs is always expressed in one's readiness to die for them, and the life that makes and keeps us faithful in this sense is born of the death that we are prepared to face. For someone who has woken to the Way, dying serves Life—and only the inner master has authority to demand this kind of dying of us.

The glow of a greater Life lies over death. Another Life speaks in its silence, and limitless vistas lie beyond the barrier that it seemingly rears across our path. It is only by sensing death within us that we can also feel the *Life* to which it already points.

Heroism and resignation are the two qualities that allow humans either to conquer death triumphantly or to accept it in painful abnegation without going beyond their normal limits. These are the ways in which death is reflected in the ego that sees no further than this world and deploys its courage and altruism on this side of the barrier. It is only when humans have experienced their true roots beyond the barrier that death puts them in touch with the other, wholly different and limitless dimension, and becomes the door leading home to their eternal origin.

People who have "died" and come back—who have, in other words, been briefly "on the other side"—all speak of experiencing a pure, blissful, redeeming light. What is this light, if not the light that sometimes pierces the curtain of ordinary consciousness? But our alienation from Being and our total concentration on the visible, comprehensible world prevent us from seeing it. The daylight of this world seems to blind us to the starlight of the world beyond, and it is only by allowing ordinary consciousness to darken that we can at last see the light of Life.

Death's meaning changes at every stage in the process of becoming.

At the first stage, it is merely a dark threat to life, and must be resisted. But its darkness also serves as a background and throws all the bright pleasures of existence, of life secured and recovered, into brilliant relief. Death is not simply a constant threat but also the constant renewer of our joy in living—indeed, it is the secret knowledge of death that first gives life its radiance. Every moment lived without fear is bathed in a joy that only death's presence allows us to feel.

At the second stage, we move on to serving others and to "work"—and death is the sacrifice we are prepared to make in doing so. Readiness to die in a cause is the basis of life at this stage. Physical death may be the supreme sacrifice that anyone can make in life's service—and the whole of life itself can be lived as a sacrifice in the service of others.

At the third stage, death becomes the threshold to a higher life. This is what it means when we wake to the Way—in it and through it we experience Life that waits for us to become mediums so that it can manifest itself in the world. For its sake we are also prepared to give up everything we clung to at the first stage, and everything we selflessly served and created at the second. Death now becomes our teacher and friend on the Way, leads us on, and opens the door into another *Life*—while we are still in this one.

The meaning we find in life cannot be separated from the meaning we give death. Seen from the outside, death is an end—from the inside, a beginning. Properly died, death is total release: letting ourselves go, letting ourselves sink, letting ourselves fade into nothingness and fuse with the fullness of eternity. And from this merging with the primal ground of Being, which we ourselves basically are, there rises—if we will only let it do so—our true nature. Death becomes birth, darkness turns to light, and, by surrendering the present and actual, we make room for the future and possible. This pattern of change is the underlying formula of all true meditation. It is only when all thoughts and images fall silent that we hear the master's voice.

The more fully we die to our natural ego, the more clearly we appear in our true nature. The more we merge with our individual true nature, the more we encounter *universal true nature* in ourselves. Allowing the ego that cares about permanence to die brings us into contact with Life. The more we turn away from the world-conditioned ego and find ourselves as individuals, the more we can sense universal, supra-individual Life. And so death of the ego can bring us face to face with the true nature and Life of all things. It is only by uniting ourselves with this Life that we can develop the true ego that transcends the world and is yet able to strive, create, and love in the world in a manner that accords with true nature.

The truth of anything said about death, like the truth of anything said about human reality, is limited by the consciousness from which it comes. The natural ego's vision of reality is the narrowest of all, since it limits our reality to what we feel, perceive, and understand—where we are and when we are. The time we have is completed, fulfilled, and exhausted between birth and death. Anything beyond this is assumption, speculation, fantasy, metaphysics, wishful thinking, or nightmare. Are we then to conclude that Life beyond life and death is a pious belief and nothing else? No! It is age-old experience and knowledge: knowledge—rooted in experience of the deepest kind, born of expanded consciousness, and secured in a millennial tradition—of the transcendent and divine ground, origin, and meaning of our lives. The experience and knowledge of Life have always been the theme of revelation, the inspiration of prophets, and the goal of those who seek God—and have always been bound up with death of *the* life that hides Life from view.

The eternity shining out in death is not permanence—not the finite in infinite series—but a reality at right angles to finitude. The enemy of Life is lying when he tries to persuade us that we cannot perceive anything beyond the here-and-now. The devil uses objective consciousness to delude us into taking seriously only those things we can pin down and define. Life, of course, cannot be pinned down. Objective consciousness is a false path, but also a natural part of the indirect route that leads us to the Way, and this means that we cannot free ourselves of it until we have reached an advanced stage in our development.

As prisoners of the worldly ego, we are doomed to forget that our origin is twofold and that we belong to two worlds. As children of earth, we belong to the contingent, limited, here-and-now world—but as children of heaven we also belong to transcendent, absolute, and limitless Being. In the world of the natural ego, everything has a beginning and an end. In the world of true nature, there are no beginnings and no ends, no births and no deaths. Every life in this world has its death. But the great Life within our true nature lies beyond life and death. Waking to the Way means remembering our twofold origin and hearing the promising, challenging voice that summons us to the life-form that unites heaven and earth in a third dimension.

Fearing death, like loving life, is a natural part of being human. It is only knowing what it is to fear death that gives us the ability and right to intuit and experience the kind of life that awaits us in death. Even worldly life, which is constantly threatened by death, never shines more brightly or gives us greater happiness than when death has brushed it: when we recover from serious illness, escape mortal danger, or emerge unscathed from battle. In peace or in war, it is only against the dark background of death that we can experience the radiance of natural life. But natural life must die before supernatural Life can shine out, and only the imminence of death can reveal the supernatural even in the natural.

All change depends on things that have come to be ceasing to be. But it is only when our human consciousness expands beyond its natural limits that we can sense something of the miracle constantly present and active within us—like an agency outside time that transforms everything within it. We are not truly ourselves until otherworldly Being's potential comes to inner consciousness through all worldly actualities— if only for an instant—and we sense what Meister Eckhart calls "the uncreated in the soul." When this happens, the invisible is at work in our visible actions. Without our doing anything, it is the unformed in us that comes to and passes out of form and, in so doing, generates the right process of becoming.

An animal does not die like a human being. Its life simply stops and is finished. This is not the kind of death we human beings want. We want to die consciously; we also fight death all the way. We do not want simply to vanish, and we reject the whole notion of an end. Wanting to last, survive, and remain is deeply rooted in our ego-nature. This is the nature that makes us define and determine everything we see, and thus hold on to ourselves in fixtures, too, seeking security and reassurance in things that last and do not change. Permanence means peace, and anything that threatens it, such as change, is hostile. But this kind of peace is, in fact, the stillness of death, where all movement ceases. The stillness of life, on the other hand, is the state in which nothing is left to impede further change.

Our *true nature* is the mode in which Life is born into us as our *Way*—an innate, infused, and necessary series of stages on the path to a life-form in which Life can increasingly reveal itself in our worldly existence. We must find the way to our true nature (wake to our own way) before we can attain our own truth. This truth—the truth of our true nature—is one of Life's modes, and this means that it is also *the* truth in the language of our particular humanity. But the fullness of Being cannot open from true nature as way, truth, and life until self-willed ego-nature, which has lost contact with its origins, disappears. In its death and in the pain that accompanies it, the new is preparing to enter inner consciousness.

Age-old tradition makes the natural human being the most perfectly disguised and encoded embodiment of the absolute reality that is actually within him. This absolute reality lives in all of us as a secret urge to self-manifestation, an unquenchable longing for something totally different and beyond the world, the uncomprehended call to a definite process of becoming, and the primal anguish of being human—and thus "apart and alone." Our original destiny is to allow Being, which we embody, to manifest itself humanly—that is, consciously and freely. But the carapace of world-ego consciousness prevents us from doing this. The eternal question is: How can we obey the living impulse of the Absolute within us? How can we attain the life that we ourselves are in in the depths of our true nature? The eternal answer is: Only by dying! Only the prisoner of world-ego registers this as a threat. Anyone who has woken to the Way sees it as the natural precondition of a state of mind and being in which the Absolute can break through, and thus as something filled with promise because it holds the key to experience of the Great Light.

Anyone who is seeking Life and whose only ambition, living or dying, is to be in Life and serve it, sees death as a friendly release from all those urges to permanence that obstruct its all-transforming movement. Dying—that moment when death, which is always at work, approaches its goal—is the prelude to the "supreme moment" of union with Life. We cannot realize too soon that this time has already come, and that death has been at work from the beginning, secretly and softly loosening our ties with the world. The death that does this is brother, not enemy, and it carries us over the ultimate threshold.

Death, we are told, is the wages of sin! This does not mean that because you have sinned you must die. What it means is that those who "stand apart," withdraw their consciousness from the stream of everlasting change, and set their own will to permanence against the law of Life, will themselves experience the ceasing-to-be that forms part of all life as "death." Because they are focused on remaining what they are, look for permanence, and try to make the transient eternal, they will inevitably experience the ceasing-to-be that is part of Life's pattern as something terrifying.

If those who start by seeing death as the ultimate, inevitable blind alley nonetheless hear, in their first contact with it, the voice of the Life into which it is trying to draw them home, this may come as the watershed experience—and show them that their fear of death is really fear of the force with which a greater Life bursts from them in death and shatters their earthly shell.

Works Cited

DÜRCKHEIM, KARLFRIED GRAF. *Erlebnis und Wandlung* [Experience and Tranformation]. Bern/ Munich: O. W. Barth-Verlag, 1982.

————. *Hara: The Vital Centre of Man*. Translated by Sylvia-Monica von Kospoth and Estelle Healey. London: Unwin Paperbacks, 1977.

————. *Überweltiches Leben in der Welt* [Other Worldly Things Living in the World]. 2d ed. Munich: O. W. Barth-Verlag, 1972.

————. *The Way of Transformation: Daily Life as a Spiritual Exercise*. Translated by Ruth Lewinnek and P. L. Travers. London: Unwin Paperbacks, 1980.

————. *Zen and Us*. Translated by Vincent Nash. New York: E. P. Dutton, 1987.

EVOLA, J. "Über das Initiatische" ["On Initiation"]. *Antaios*, vol. VI/2 (1964).

GEBSER, JEAN. *The Ever-Present Origin*. Athens: Ohio University Press, 1985.

GOVINDA, LAMA ANAGARIKA. "Durchbruch zur Transzendenz" ["Breakthrough to Transcendence"]. In *Transzendenz als Erfahrung*, edited by M. Hippius. Weilheim: O. W. Barth-Verlag, 1966.

————. *Der Weg der Weissen Wolken* [The Way of the White Clouds] Munich: O. W. Barth-Verlag.

HIPPIUS, MARIA. "Am Faden von Zeit und Ewigkeit" ["The Thread of Time and Eternity"]. In *Transzendenz als Erfahrung*, edited by M. Hippius. Weilheim: O. W. Barth-Verlag, 1966.

————. "Beitrag aus der Werkstatt" ["Contribution from the Workshop"]. In *Transzendenz als Erfahrung*, edited by M. Hippius. Weilheim: O. W. Barth-Verlag, 1966.

KLAGES, LUDWIG. *Der Geist als Widersacher der Seele* [The Spirit from the Soul's Enemy]. Leipzig: J. A. Barth, 1929.

OTTO, W. F. *Menschengestalt und Tanz* [Human Figure and Dance]. Munich: Rinn, 1956.

TRÜB, H. *Heilung aus der Begegnung* [Encounter Healing], eds. Michel and Sborowitz. Stuttgart: Klett, 1951.

VETTER, A. *Personale Anthropologie: Aufriss der humanen Struktur* [Personal Anthropology: Outline of the Human Form]. Munich/Freiburg: Alber, 1966.

WELZIG, W. *Beispielhafte Figuren* [Exemplary Figures]. Graz/Cologne: Böhlau, 1963.